Wild Flo

C000257703

John Bowler   Emma Grant
Charlie Self   Simon Wellock

Photographs by

John Bowler   Freddie Everett
Lynne Farrell   Lorne Gill
Emma Grant   Neil MacKinnon
Tony Oliver   Sarah Rose
Simon Wellock   Doug Young

Illustrations by

Val Conway

Cinquefoil Publishing, Isle of Coll

First published in the UK in 2008 by Cinquefoil Publishing

Drimcruy
Isle of Coll
Argyll
PA78 6TB

ISBN 978 0 9558202 0 5

Design by Tony Oliver
Produced by Coll Digital, Isle of Coll
Printed by Fast Print Network

Editor and project manager: Emma Grant

Editorial consultant: Lynne Farrell

Main authors: John Bowler, Emma Grant, Charlie Self, Simon Wellock

Other contributors: B and Kenneth Cassels, An Iodhlann (Tiree's historical centre), Lynne Farrell, Mairi Hedderwick, Archie Sproat, Catriona Young

Photographers: John Bowler, Freddie Everett, Lynne Farrell, Lorne Gill, Emma Grant, Neil MacKinnon, Tony Oliver, Sarah Rose, Simon Wellock, Doug Young

Illustrator: Val Conway

Maps: Tony Oliver

Proofreaders: Lynne Farrell, Barbara Jones, Carolyn Brodie Mackay, Seonaid Maclean-Bristol, Julianna Nicholls, Caroline Strachan

Thanks to Claudia Ferguson-Smyth for her considerable input in the early stages of the project

Other members of the steering group not mentioned above:
from Coll: Fiona Kennedy
from Tiree: Ulrike Johnson and Jane Rose

Thanks also to: An Acarsaid, on Coll, for provision of prize money for the local stories competition, Doug Young for providing Gaelic translations, Caroline Strachan for compiling the indexes, and to island caterers, Jane and Sophie Isaacson on Tiree and Frances Macintyre on Coll

Contents

Foreword by Mairi Hedderwick — 1

Maps of Coll and Tiree — 2-3

Introduction by Lynne Farrell, BSBI vice-county recorder — 4

A brief natural history by Charlie Self — 5

Habitats by Charlie Self — 7

Tiree plant walk:
route, access, map and description by John Bowler — 10

Coll plant walk:
route, access, map and description by Simon Wellock — 13

How to use this book — 16

4 easy steps to flower identification — 18

Introduction to the blue-purple section — 19

Introduction to the red-pink section — 51

The orange flower — 82

Introduction to the yellow-brown section — 83

Introduction to the green section — 120

Introduction to the white section — 127

Local stories by B and Kenneth Cassels, An Iodhlann,
Archie Sproat and Catriona Young — 171

Illustrated glossary — 175

Leaf shapes and examples — 176

Glossary — 178

Respect our islands and
Publications and websites about Tiree and Coll — 180

Recommended reading and Bibliography — 181

Index of common names — 182

Index of Latin names — 185

About the project — 187

Author and Photographer credits — 188-189

Foreword

As I write this, the heather on Coll, and no doubt Tiree, is intensely purple. Everyone is talking about the phenomenon of plant flowering on the islands, this spring and summer of '07.

I've known Coll since the '50s and '60s, when wildflower growth was not so fecund: overgrazing and rabbits took their toll. But those days are no more. Yet I can look back to that time, when my children were young, and wild-flower eating (yes!) and picking and pressing (yes!) were summer activities.

I am no botanist, as you can tell. I am therefore very honoured to be asked to introduce this professional botanical record of Coll and Tiree. Tho' long thralled to Coll, I am also delighted to have this opportunity to admit that it was on a summer tapestried machair at Vaul on Tiree that I first stood in awe and was seduced by all things Hebridean.

One of my trades is as a writer for children. Toddler walks along the slow Totronald road and meanders into the machair and bents at Crossapol all those years ago were subconscious source material for my work. The plants that meaningfully marked our forays into a wider world beyond home became botanical references that subsequently filtered into the illustrations for the Katie Morag stories. Look, and you will see!

How convenient, the docken leaves for vigorous salve so near to the nettles; bunches of bog-myrtle to flagellate the flies; soorag leaves (sorrel) to sweetly chew; clover honey to suck; groundnuts (pignut) at Feall to dig up and crunch – all keeping hunger at bay. The rosehip syrup I once made was not appreciated, but maybe I had the wrong recipe. In the autumn, the dried bracken was taken home for the hens' nests.

But it was not all rape and pillage. The bank of primroses on the Totronald road (still there and dramatically more dense) was never touched. Well, maybe a few for the little vase in the kitchen and a couple of flag iris for the bigger jug...

I know that this distinctively local and timely publication will educate, inform and celebrate the bonny diversity of the flora of our islands for generations to come.

I hope our long-distant, and innocent, depredations are forgiven.

Mairi Hedderwick
Isle of Coll '07

To Barra

1 Balevullin
2 Balemartine
3 Balephetrish Bay
4 Beinn Hough
5 Ceann a' Mhara
6 Caolas
7 Cornaigmore
8 Crossapol
9 Gott Bay
10 Hynish
11 Kenovay
12 Kilkenneth
13 Loch a' Phuill
14 Loch Bhasapol
15 Loch Riaghain
16 Moss
17 Ruaig
18 Salum
19 Sandaig
20 Scarinish
21 Sorobaidh Bay
22 Tràigh Bhaigh
23 Tràigh Bhi
24 The Reef
25 Vaul

Isle of Tiree

Isle of Coll

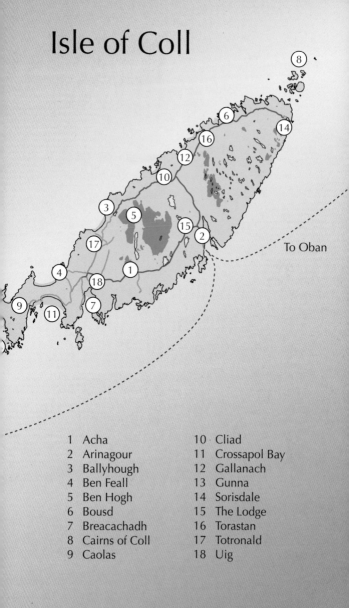

1	Acha	10 Cliad
2	Arinagour	11 Crossapol Bay
3	Ballyhough	12 Gallanach
4	Ben Feall	13 Gunna
5	Ben Hogh	14 Sorisdale
6	Bousd	15 The Lodge
7	Breacachadh	16 Torastan
8	Cairns of Coll	17 Totronald
9	Caolas	18 Uig

To Oban

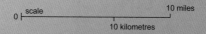

scale
0   10 miles

10 kilometres

Map reproduced by the kind permission of The Ordnance Survey
from their 1:63360 map of Coll and Tiree.

Introduction

I have visited these islands for over 30 years and have always been impressed by their wonderful variety of natural history, their colourscapes, and the traditions and welcome of the local people. In 1996 I became the Botanical Society of the British Isles (BSBI) official vice-county recorder for Mid Ebudes, which consists of Tiree, Coll and Mull, and all the smaller islands around them. This is something I have never regretted.

There have been other recorders, and many visiting and local botanists. Several magazines and books published about the islands have made people more aware of these special places. The previous folk who have contributed to the increasing knowledge are Symers M Macvicar, John William Heslop-Harrison, Joan Clark, Agnes Walker, B and Kenneth Cassels, and, more recently, David Pearman and Chris Preston, who wrote 'A Flora of Tiree, Gunna and Coll', published in 2000. This book provides a full account of all the wild flowers on the islands, but it is essentially a scientific work and does not have illustrations.

So we come to the present work, which began when I was on Coll in Fiona Kennedy's shop, discussing books and plants. 'What we need is a colourful guide to the plants of the islands with plenty of pictures', said Fiona. I agreed, but as I was fully employed at that time, I said it would take me several years to complete. 'We need it sooner' was the response. Then along came Emma Grant with a proposal for a Nàdair project and the energy to turn this into a reality. With the help of many people, both on and off the islands, the guide is now complete, and I hope it will inform and encourage you all to enjoy and learn more about the wild flowers of Coll and Tiree.

Lynne Farrell
BSBI vice-county recorder for vascular plants

If you wish to send me any records or notes about the plants, please do so to:-
Lynne Farrell, BSBI vice-county recorder,
41 High Street, Hemingford Grey, Cambs. PE28 9BJ

A brief natural history

The bones of Coll and Tiree are made from an exceedingly ancient, hard and acidic rock, called 'Lewisian Gneiss' – named from Lewis

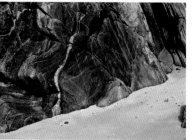

and pronounced 'nice'. For 3,000 million years (yes, count them!) these stones have literally been our bedrock, underpinning the islands while they were under the sea, under the ice, at the equator, or connected to Greenland.

Lewisian Gneiss

With these bones bare after the retreat of the last ice age, only 10–15,000 years ago, the very nature of these stones - coupled with the mild, wet and windy climate, and the bounty of the sea - have determined which plants can grow and where.

Since the ice melted, two very different processes have shaped the islands' main habitats: on the one hand, wet acidic soils known as podsols have formed from the eroded bedrock, and in places peat has built up - sometimes several metres thick - spreading over the land like a soggy blanket, making a melancholy place of bog cotton and haunting bird cries; on the other we are blessed with shell-sand (crushed sea-

shells) that have been cast ashore by the Atlantic swells and blown inland by winter gales. Shell sand creates a habitat opposite to that of peat and podsol, one that is dry and alkaline: a light and heady place, where you can lie down in clover and be lifted up by the joy of skylarks. And of course the peat and the shell-sand blend together

Shell-sand

in every conceivable mix, so here, on an intimate scale, we can find plants that love wet or dry, acid or alkaline, or anything in between.

Into this plant heaven came people. First, the Mesolithic hunter-gatherers, about 8,000 years ago, who left us their shards of flint, stone tools, and shell middens. Then, a succession of Neolithic, Bronze Age, and Iron Age peoples, who first introduced farming and left their mark on the land with standing stones, crannogs, forts and brochs. On the highway of the sea many others came and stayed, as they do to this day: the Picts; the Celts; the Vikings; the Clans and the Crofters. For thousands of years Coll and Tiree have been inhabited, and the islands have provided all that their people needed.

We need food, shelter, warmth, clothing and medicines to sustain ourselves, just as the Vikings did, just as the hunter-gatherers of long ago did. These islands have provided it all, and more, principally through the plants that grow here. From marram and heather for thatching

Thatched cottage, Tiree

houses, to peat for fuel; from nettles for fibres to make string and cloth, to the myriad leaves, shoots, roots and berries for food, and iris rhizomes for sore throats and toothache: everything we need is out there - only the loss of the traditional knowledge will keep it from us.

Low intensity farming and crofting - through seasonal cattle grazing, growing crops without herbicides, and cutting hay - has developed further mosaics of land use onto the gneiss/peat/shell sand matrix, enhancing the opportunities for plants to thrive.

These long geological, climatic and cultural developments have given us these Hebridean jewels. From the tiny, sticky, sundew catching midges in a bog, to the riot of orchids in the dunes, there is hardly a corner of these two islands where the sights and smells of wild and beautiful flowers do not raise the spirit and make us grateful.

Standing stone, Tiree

Charlie Self

Habitats

To aid identification of the flowers in this book we have assigned a habitat category to each: **Coastal**, **Grassland**, **Heath**, or **Wetland**. To distinguish, for example, Heath Bedstraw from Common Marsh-bedstraw, note whether the plant is in a Heath or Wetland habitat, and you're almost there.

A word of caution: the four basic habitat types of Coastal, Grassland, Heath or Wetland can be infinitely variable and intimately jumbled. The transitions between dunes, machair, dry grassland, wet grassland and wetland are subjective, subtle and very beautiful. The landscape of the islands is like a finely woven tapestry of habitat mosaics.

 Coastal

The coastal zone is where plants have to cope with intense exposure to the salty sea and is a difficult place to put down roots.

- **Sandy beaches**: made predominately of shell sand. Sea Rocket and oraches may be found on the strandline, the high tide mark.
- **Shingle and pebble beaches**: might not have the wow factor of the sandy beaches, but they will if you find the rare Oysterplant.
- **Rocky shores**: make up the majority of the Coastal zone where the ancient land fronts the restless sea. A place for Thrift.

Sea Rocket

- **Sea cliffs**: such as Ceann a' Mhara or Ben Feall - provide inaccessible ledges, where plants such as Roseroot thrive.
- **Salt marshes**: fringe the few sheltered inlets such as Loch Breacachadh, where scurvy grasses, Thrift, and rare eyebrights grow low in the short turf.

Machair

 Grassland

Grasslands are the backbone of the floral and agricultural communities. This is where the habitats determine what the farmers and crofters can do, and vice versa: what the farmers and crofters do determines how well the flowers thrive.

- **Dunes and Machair**: formed from shell sand blown inland. Steep young dunes near the sea are covered with Marram; dune slacks are damp hollows full of orchids; older and flatter machair is further inland and is a botanist's paradise.
- **Inbye**: comprises the most fertile and cropped fields, in by the croft or farm. These fields are sometimes grazed, sometimes left as meadows to be cut for hay, and sometimes used for a cereal crop.
- **Sliabh**: is the Gaelic term for the usually wetter and more acidic grasslands that occur inland, away from the influence of the shell sand.

 Heath

Sometimes known as moorland, Heath is the land of the heathers.

- **Dry heath**: occurs on the acidic bedrock and is extensive, predominately covered with Heather and Bell Heather.
- **Wet heath**: where drainage is poor and peat has built up. Wet heath develops with Cross-leaved Heath and sphagnum mosses.

Heather on heath

◉ Wetland

Unsurprisingly, as this is the west of Scotland, wetlands are a common habitat, but varied and important.

- **Bog/Marsh**: when you walk through wet heath and suddenly the water seeps over your boots, then you are in a bog. Bogs tend to be very peaty and acidic, with plants such as the insectivorous sundews, while marshes tend to be less acidic with plants such as Yellow Iris and Common Reed.
- **Open water**: from acid hill lochs with Water Lobelia and White Water-lily, to machair lochs, rich with submerged pondweeds, the chemistry of the water - derived from the underlying rocks or sand - determines the characteristic plants.
- **Ditches**: are certainly not dull. The juxtaposition of dryer banks and still or flowing water creates a mini-world of possibilities for plants such as Brookweed, Branched Bur-reed and Meadowsweet.

Wetland

Woodland is no longer a major habitat type on the islands. The branches and stumps preserved in the peat on Coll show that woodlands were extensive long ago. Now, only fragments remain, although groves of Aspen, banks of Willow, even occasional Oak, Rowan, Birch and Common Juniper can be found tucked into crevices on Coll, whilst low-growing willows and a few wind-sculpted Hawthorns survive on Tiree. Older plantings of Lodgepole Pine and Sycamore have been added to recently by small-scale native woodland plantations.

Charlie Self

Tiree plant walk
Tràigh Bhi and Ceann a' Mhara

This walk covers examples of the four main habitats, allowing the casual observer to see a wide range of flowering plants within a relatively short distance (total length of round trip is 4-5km). A shorter return route is possible, if the walker does not wish to head up onto the headland of Ceann a' Mhara itself, by simply turning back from the lower slopes of the hill.

Timing: different plants flower through the summer, so it is not possible to see everything on one visit. However, a wide variety of flowers can be seen between May and September, with the best displays in June-July.

Access: park in the designated car park immediately after the pumping station at Balephuil (NL954410) and proceed on foot. Alternatively, park off the road at Balephuil and walk to the south end of the beach via the gate at NL956403. On no account drive through the dunes, which are a protected area, and avoid approaching stock, particularly during lambing/calving periods. Dogs must be kept

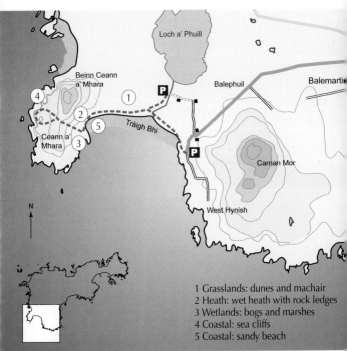

1 Grasslands: dunes and machair
2 Heath: wet heath with rock ledges
3 Wetlands: bogs and marshes
4 Coastal: sea cliffs
5 Coastal: sandy beach

Map reproduced by the kind permission of The Ordnance Survey from their 1:63360 map of Coll and Tiree

under control (ideally on a lead if stock are likely to be present). For your own safety, DO NOT cross the fence that borders the western sea cliffs of Ceann a' Mhara.

Route: from the car park, follow the track on foot SW across the dunes, keeping the ditch on your left, until you reach the edge of the beach. Proceed westwards along the edge of the dunes on a series of small stock trails through the Marram grass. The dunes and neighbouring grazed machair hold a wide range of typical machair flowers.

Continue for just under a kilometre until you reach the rising ground at the end of the beach. The steep rock ledges on the landwards side of the path hold a range of interesting plants, including Bluebell and Primrose in April-May and Bloody Crane's-bill in July. Skirt south of the steepest slopes and then proceed west up the hill, heading towards the low col between the two main hills on the headland. The lower slopes have wet flushes with a range of wetland plants, whilst adjacent rocky slopes have different plants growing amongst the short grass swards on the thinner soil.

Continue through the col to reach the west side of the headland and view the dramatic sea cliffs from the landward side of the fence. Binoculars are handy for scanning the ledges to look for some specialised cliff plants, which include Red Campion, Bluebell and Sea Campion. An alternative return route is to walk back along the beach itself, which presents the opportunity of seeing one or two additional plants above the strandline.

Grasslands: dunes and machair; the vegetation along the track to the dunes is closely grazed by stock, but common flowers include the familiar Daisy, Red and White Clover, Silverweed and Common Bird's-foot-trefoil. The seaward dunes are dominated by tough Marram grass that was once harvested extensively for the roofs of thatched houses on the island. Careful searching may reveal the odd plant of Sea-holly – a rarity on the island. As you head west along the back of the beach, the dunes merge with the machair and further common plants to look for include Lady's Bedstraw,

Tràigh Bhì

Red Bartsia, Yarrow, Wild Carrot and Eyebright, as well as more conspicuous Creeping Thistle. Less obvious plants include Common and Sea Mouse-ears, Meadow and Bulbous Buttercups and hawkbit species, and more locally Kidney Vetch, Lesser Meadow-rue and Groundsel.

Heath: wet heath with rock ledges; the steep rocky slopes at the west end of the beach hold a number of interesting plants, particularly on ledges that are inaccessible to grazing sheep. There is a fine display of Bluebells, Primroses and Lesser Celandine in spring, whilst in July the Bloody Crane's-bill flowers on just a few steep cliffs. More frequent are Selfheal, Wild Thyme, Heath Milkwort and Tormentil amongst the short turf, with Spring Squill frequent in May and a few Field Gentians and Harebells later in the summer. Scarcer plants to hunt for here include Common Centaury and Purple Milk-vetch. Large numbers of Heath Spotted-orchids are present in June and there are local patches of Heather, Bell Heather and Cross-leaved Heath.

Wetlands: bogs and marshes; the damp marshy areas on the flanks of the hill are dominated by a range of sedges and cotton grass, together with dense beds of Yellow Iris. These areas harbour a wide range of plants that are typical of damp conditions. Ragged-Robin, Marsh Ragwort and Bog Pimpernel are common lower down, whilst Bog Asphodel is more numerous higher up the slope. Orchids include both Early and Northern Marsh-orchids in June, together with more numerous Common Spotted-orchids. Less conspicuous flowers include Marsh Willowherb, Marsh Lousewort, Tufted Forget-me-not, Marsh Pennywort and Lesser Spearwort in the streams.

Bluebells

Coastal: sea cliffs; the impressive sea cliffs of Ceann a' Mhara host a range of salt-tolerant plants that are easily viewed in safety through binoculars or by looking over the fence. Thrift is widespread on the rocks, whilst the cliff-top turf holds giant flowering heads of Wild Angelica, as well as Common Sorrel and Tormentil amidst a low forest of Creeping Willow. Red Campion flowers in the gullies amongst Bluebell, Sea Mayweed and more locally Sea Campion.

Coastal: sandy beach; a few additional plants can be found along the top of the sandy beach, above the strandline. These include dense patches of Sea Sandwort plus occasional plants of Babington's Orache.

John Bowler

Coll plant walk
Totronald

This walk covers examples of the four main habitats, allowing the visitor to see a wide range of flowering plants within a distance of 2-3km.

Timing: plants flower at different times through the summer, so it is not possible to see everything on one visit. However, a wide variety can be seen between May and September, with the best displays in June-July.

Access: park in the RSPB car park immediately north of Totronald and proceed on foot. On no account drive through the dunes,

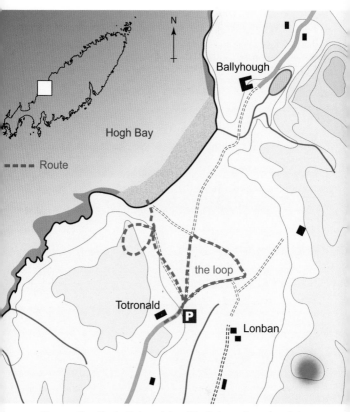

Map reproduced by the kind permission of The Ordnance Survey from their 1:63360 map of Coll and Tiree

which are a protected area, and avoid approaching livestock, particularly during lambing/calving periods. Dogs must be kept under control.

Route: walk back up the road for 50m and stop at the gate to the field on the right with the ruined building. A good selection of commoner grassland species such as buttercups, speedwells, and forget-me-nots can be seen from here, without having to enter the field and disturb the breeding corncrakes. It is also a great place to see an array of orchids, particularly Common Spotted and some of its enormous hybrids.

From here, head back down the road towards the car park, stopping just short of it to view the flowers along the stream to the left. Go through the gate and turn right following the fence line. The inbye (meadow) to your right is filled with wild flowers and the heavy scent is memorable. Amongst the commoner species, things to look out for are the crimson red *coccinea* subspecies of Early Marsh-orchid, alongside its pink nominate form, whilst the wetter areas of the field are alive with wetland plants such as Cuckooflower, Ragged-Robin, Yellow Iris and Marsh-marigold.

You can now do a loop across the machair grassland and dunes, which hold a wide range of typical machair flowers, including a carpet of Bloody Crane's-bill and thousands of Pyramidal and Frog Orchids. Rocky outcrops covered with Wild Thyme and Bird's-foot-trefoil are worth a closer look, for species such as Common Centaury and Field Gentian, whilst the wetter dune slacks are good places to look for Northern Marsh-orchids.

Wild Thyme and Lady's Bedstraw

Hogh beach

After taking the loop, head back to the gate by the car park and from here, head up the hill to the west, following the grass track. Continue up and over for just under a kilometre until you reach the top of the hill with its stunning views of the beach, Hogh Bay and the Outer Hebrides. You should see a gate on your left which leads to an area of heath. Remember this, as you will return here shortly, but first, continue along the track down to the beach. Check above the strandline for typical beach species such as Babington's Orache and Sea Rocket and the rocky shore to the left for Thrift and Sea Mayweed.

From the shore, head back up the hill and through the gate into the heath. The steep rock ledges hold a range of interesting plants, including English Stonecrop, Bluebell and Primrose. The wet flushes near the gate are good for a range of wetland species, including Grass-of-Parnassus, Lesser Spearwort, Marsh Lousewort, Butterwort and sundews, whilst in the grassy areas

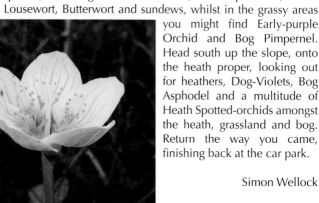

you might find Early-purple Orchid and Bog Pimpernel. Head south up the slope, onto the heath proper, looking out for heathers, Dog-Violets, Bog Asphodel and a multitude of Heath Spotted-orchids amongst the heath, grassland and bog. Return the way you came, finishing back at the car park.

Simon Wellock

Grass-of-Parnassus

How to use this book

This book is intended to be useful for all ages and a range of abilities, from the absolute beginner to the more knowledgeable plant-seeker.

Common names have been taken from *English Names of Wild Flowers* published by the Botanical Society of the British Isles*.

Latin name

This gives a general description of where you will find the flower within the general habitats. For more information on habitats see page 7.

This gives a general description and notes any distinguishing characteristics or similar species.

Gives standard statistical information covering:
Plant form: gives the form (erect, trailing etc) and a range of heights. As for flowering times, this can vary greatly from year to year and between the islands. The statistics in brackets have been lifted from *New Flora of the British Isles* by Clive Stace*. Otherwise, those given are specifically for Coll and Tiree, where the size is generally smaller than would be found on the mainland.
Flowers: gives the length or width of the flowers or flower-heads.
Leaves: gives the arrangement, shape and features such as toothed or hairy.

Shows the plant in its natural environment.

This indicates the general type of habitat. For more information on habitats see page 7.

⬭ Coastal

◍ Grassland

◍ Heath

◍ Wetland

This indicates the status of the plant as indicated in *The Vascular Plant Red Data List for Great Britain**.

This indicates the family to which the plant belongs.

Oysterplant *Mertensia m...*

Habitat: rare, occurs only on beaches. Currently o Tiree, and a few scat

An unusual low-growing of coarse sand and shingle small, deep blue flowers clustered at the end of the tr stems, and are initially pi slowly turning a deep p blue. The distinctive grey- leaves are rubbery and rou texture, with a hard point tip and a pronounced c vein. The thick fleshy s become tinged purple with

Form:	trailing,
Flowers:	up to 6m
Leaves:	oval to t

A scarce plant that is sporad in numbers. Colonies can p competed by other salt-tole requires storms from time t exploit. The rubbery leaves The Gaelic translates as 'gif

36 Borage family

16

Gaelic names have been taken from *Ainmean Gaidhlig Lusan* by Clark and MacDonald* and checked by locals. It is understood that there are varying names from island to island. We have done our best to be as accurate as possible.

lac na Mara

ear the top of sheltered
ation at a single site in north
SW Coll.

The book is divided into five colour categories. A beginner can immediately narrow the range of their search with knowledge of only the flower colour. It should be noted that plants are listed under their predominant colour, so a Daisy will appear under white although it also has yellow and pink.

Covers selected information, for example herbal use, use as a dye, or any other quirky stories of interest.

g.

mm across.

, up to 8cm long.

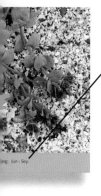

e and generally declining
years, but are slowly out-
stable shingle. The plant
de fresh shingle habitat to
taste a little like oysters!

Gives months as to when the plant is in flower. In some cases the plant is noteworthy when displaying leaves only or seeds. In these cases the months for these are also indicated. It should be noted that this is a rough guide only as the flowering times can vary from year to year and from island to island depending on weather and grazing systems.

Any words appearing in **bold** are further explained in the illustrated and written glossaries on pages 175-179.

When using the index, you will notice that some of the plants appear in parentheses. This indicates that the plant has a passing reference within another plant's account, but does not have a full account to itself. In a few cases we have simplified our botanical descriptions. For example, the difference between petals and sepals in a Yellow Iris is not highlighted. We have assumed that once you get to that level of understanding, you'll be looking at a different book!

ng: Jun - Sep

*see recommended reading, page 181

4 easy steps to flower identification

This is not meant to be a scientific key, but if you follow these steps, in most cases you will only be looking at a few pages to identify your flower rather than flicking through the entire book!

1. Establish the colour of your flower and turn to the relevant colour section
- Please be aware that colour definition is subjective: one person's pink is another person's light purple.
- If you are not sure about the colour, have a look at the introduction to each colour section. You may find some useful pointers there.

2. Estimate the size of the flower-head or individual flower
- Flowers are listed roughly from largest to smallest within their groups of flower colour.
- Therefore, in the yellow-brown section, Yellow Iris appears before Dandelion, which appears before the buttercups, which appears before Tormentil.
- The size of the flower-heads will vary slightly from season to season, so this is not an exact science, but should give you a general help within the colour section. If it is a big flower look at the beginning. If it is very small check towards the end!
- Check the statistics box for size of flower-head to see if you are in the right ball park… also check the size of your plant overall.

3. Check the flowering times
- At the bottom of each page you will see months indicating the flowering times (plus times for seeds or leaves only if this is particularly relevant).

4. Still confused? You need to become aware of your habitat and/or start looking at leaves
- At the bottom of the page are symbols indicating in which of the four main habitats the flower occurs.
- At the top of each page there is a verbal description of the sorts of places you are likely to see the flower.
- Each page contains a statistics section with basic information on leaf size.

Please note: height of plants, size of flowers and flowering times are all rough indicators which can vary from island to island and year to year depending on weather conditions and grazing regimes.

For further help on how to use this book, please turn to page 16.

Introduction to the blue-purple section

When looking at the blue-purple section, it is worth keeping in mind that one person's light purple might be another person's pink. Some flowers would happily sit in both colour categories, so it is as well to keep an open mind. The beautiful Oysterplant is initially pink, but, as it spends the majority of its flowering life as blue-purple, it resides in the blue-purple section. You will see a number of orchids in this section. They are notorious for hybridising and thus making the process of identification even more difficult. We would recommend that enthusiasts in this field refer to specific orchid books, such as *Wild Orchids of Scotland*, by Brian Allan and Patrick Woods.

Although this is principally a wild flower book, we have included some anomalies. Common Reed is one such plant: it is a grass, but one with conspicuous flower-heads. The decisions about what to include or not were influenced by what we thought people would see in their travels around our beautiful isles, rather than strict adherence to a category.

On certain days, when the light is right, you may enjoy seeing the various purple hues of this section being mirrored by the colours of neighbouring islands on the horizon.

Oysterplant

Purple-loosestrife *Lythrum salicaria*/Lus na Sìochaint

Habitat: locally frequent in ditches and marshes.

A very tall, late-summer flowering plant with a blaze of deep purple flowers in tightly **whorled spikes**. Each flower has five narrow petals, which are tissue thin and crumpled in appearance. The tough, erect stem is square in shape, with ridges at the corners. It bears stalkless leaves in **opposite** pairs higher up and in **whorls** of three lower down. The similar Marsh Woundwort (page 27) and the rare Common Hemp-nettle have much pinker flowers, which are hooded above and have a patterned lower **lip**.

Form:	**erect**, up to 150cm.
Flowers:	up to 15mm across.
Leaves:	**opposite** or **whorled**, elongated **heart shape**, up to 15cm long.

The flower comes in three different forms in which the **style** can be shorter than, about equal to, or much longer than the **sepals**, whilst the **stamens** are equally different in length. These differences in flower structure help ensure that flowers are not fertilised by pollen from the same plant.

The Latin, 'Lythrum', is derived from the Greek for blood. Tonics made from all parts of the plant treated dysentery, internal and external bleeding, and helped heal wounds and ulcers. It is a strong-growing species that is invasive in North America.

Purple-loosestrife family

Flowering: Jul - Sep

Common Reed *Phragmites australis*/Cuilc

Habitat: occasionally abundant and dominant in ditches and around lochs, sometimes in bogs.

Common Reed is a distinctive, stout perennial grass that forms reed beds around or in wet habitats. The flowers are lovely and soft, with a purplish colour. At the top of the ligule (a small membranous flap, where the leaf joins the stem) is a dense fringe of short hairs. In winter the plants turn pale brown, and the whole reed bed becomes much more distinct in the still-green landscape.

Form:	**erect,** up to 250cm.
Flowers:	**flower-head**, up to 40cm long, loose, soft, purplish.
Leaves:	grey-green, **lance shaped**, smooth-edged, to 5cm wide.

Reed beds make very good wildlife habitats, where skulking creatures, from otters to water rails, find food and security. Loch Ballyhough, on Coll, and Loch Bhasapol, on Tiree, are excellent places to watch the waterbirds disappear and reappear from the fringe of reed beds. Common Reed was recently used on a thatched roof on Tiree to fill in some hollows where the Marram grass had sagged.

Grass family

Flowering: Jun - Sep

21

Sea-holly *Eryngium maritimum*/Cuileann Tràgha

Habitat: very local and occasional in the fore-dunes of sandy beaches in West Tiree from Tràigh Bhaigh to Balephetrish Bay, and very rarely at the west tip of Coll.

A highly distinctive plant of active sand dunes close to the shore. The tiny blue flowers are clustered in tight heads above spiky **bracts** at the end of the stiff, pale upright stems. The bluish-grey leaves are tough and waxy, and are similar in shape to those of Holly, being strongly **toothed** at the edges, with each tooth bearing a sharp spine. The leaves bear bold pale veins and become dry and crinkled with age. The upper leaves have no stalks, whereas the lower leaves have long stalks.

Form:	**erect**, up to 60cm.
Flowers:	**flower-head**, up to 3 cm across.
Leaves:	**toothed** with spines, up to 15cm long.

The sugared root of Sea-holly was popular as a sweetmeat in the 17th century, and also doubled-up as an expectorant. Sea-holly has an extensive root system which helps to stabilise the sand.

Carrot family

Flowering: Jun - Sep

Spear Thistle *Cirsium vulgare*/Cluaran Deilgneach

Habitat: common in grasslands.

The stem is branched above and is downy with interrupted spiny wings. The purple-pink **flower-heads** are solitary, or appear in loose clusters. Aside from the **flower-head** being larger than those of the similar Creeping and Marsh Thistle, the swollen flower base is more rounded and the green **bracts** with spines at their tips that arch backwards. Spear Thistle leaves are prickly to hairy on the upper side, and each lobe ends in a long stout spine, resembling the point of a spear.

No other plant has played such an important role in Scottish emblems, symbols, art, or design. The highest state honour that can be awarded is The Order of the Thistle, motto: 'Nobody attacks me with impunity'. Romantic legends of careless Viking invaders being foiled after stepping on thistles and yelling out may be the reason for its adoption as a national symbol, or maybe because it resembles the Schiltron - the massed ranks of spears that proved so effective at Bannockburn, under Robert the Bruce. In 1470 the thistle was embossed on Scottish coins, and Mary Queen of Scots incorporated it into the Great Seal of Scotland. Penetrating deep into our emotions, the thistle logo is worn proudly on rugby jerseys by the national team. In football, we have Inverness Caledonian Thistle and Partick Thistle, supporters of whom are called the Jags!

Form:	**erect,** up to 150cm.
Flowers:	**flower-head,** 3cm-5cm long, 2cm-3cm across.
Leaves:	15cm-30cm, **spear shaped**, with wavy-edged and toothed lobes.

Daisy family

Creeping Thistle *Cirsium arvense*/Fòthannan Achaidh
Marsh Thistle *Cirsium palustre*/Cluaran Lèana

Habitat: Creeping Thistle is locally abundant in dry grasslands, while Marsh Thistle is locally common in wet grasslands.

Creeping Thistle

Form: **erect**, up to 90cm, (can reach 120cm).

Flowers: **flower-head,** up to 25mm long.

Leaves: oblong to **lance shaped** with wavy-edged lobes.

The easiest way to distinguish these two thistles is by the lack of spines, hairs or wings along the stem of the Creeping Thistle. The dark red/purple flowers of Marsh Thistle appear in a crowded cluster, while the pinker flowers of Creeping Thistle form a more open cluster. Both flowers can sometimes be white. The purplish **bracts** of Marsh Thistle are pointed, but lack the spiny tips of similarly coloured Creeping Thistle. The leaves of the two species are rather different. Those of the Marsh Thistle are hairy on their upper side, with spines along the edges and tips of the lobes. The leaves are dark green, but sometimes have a purple flush. In contrast, Creeping Thistle leaves are hairless on top, but cottony below. They have strong, slender spines along their wavy edge and are grey green. Creeping Thistle is so called because it has creeping roots (**rhizomes**).

Although now considered by many to be weeds, thistles were widely used as horse or cattle fodder. They were pulled from a cut crop with wooden tongs and then crushed in mills to destroy the spines. The stems were also widely eaten by people as an early summer vegetable, with the spines removed, and the flowers have an edible heart. Both species provide important nectar sources for bumblebees, including the rare Great Yellow Bumblebee, and other insects.

Marsh Thistle

Form: **erect**, up to 150cm, (can reach 200cm).

Flowers: **flower-head,** up to 20mm long.

Leaves: narrow, deeply lobed.

Daisy family

Flowering: Jul - Sep

Common Knapweed *Centaurea nigra*/Cnapan Dubh

Habitat: frequent on dunes, pastures, machair and roadside verges.

A tall, hairy **perennial**, which branches near the top of the stem and loosely resembles a thistle (page 23). The purple-magenta **florets** project from a swollen, hard base, covered in brown bracts (thus giving it its alternate name, 'Hardheads'). The **flower-head** resembles a small, bristly pineapple. The stems are stiff and grooved and become swollen beneath the base of the **flower-head**. The upper leaves are simple, but some of the lower leaves have tooth-like points down both sides.

Form:	**erect**, 30cm-100cm.
Flowers:	**flower-head,** 2cm-4cm across.
Leaves:	**lance shaped**, lower leaves slightly lobed.

Due to its late flowering, this species is a major food source for the Great Yellow Bumblebee, particularly for the queens, which feed on its rich nectar, in preparation for hibernation. It is also attractive to migrant butterflies, such as Painted Lady and Red Admiral. It is very susceptible to increases in soil fertility and so tends to be found in old, 'unimproved' pastures that have not been artificially fertilized.

Daisy family

Flowering: Jul - Oct

25

Wild Pansy *Viola tricolor* subsp. *curtisii*/
Goimean-searradh nan Coilleag

Habitat: occasional in sand dunes and machair on Coll, though rare on Tiree.

The Wild Pansy is instantly recognisable with its single flower held up like a child's face. The five petals splay out, the lower one being broadest and elongated at the base into a **spur**. The upper petals are generally purple, while the lower one is yellow. The two side petals are often a mixture, and the colour mix of the whole flower can be variable. The leaves appear on short stalks, with leafy **stipules** in pairs at leaf base.

Form:	**erect**, up to 10cm.
Flowers:	2cm across.
Leaves:	**alternate**, oval to **heart shaped**, **toothed**.

The Wild Pansy is one of Britain's favourite plants and is held in great affection. Witness the many folk names it has: Heartsease; Love-lies-bleeding; Love-in-idleness; Love idol; Cuddle me; Call-me-to-you; Jack-jump-up-and-kiss-me; Kiss-her-in-the-buttery; Meet-me-in-the-entry. No wonder Shakespeare used it as a love charm in *A Midsummer Night's Dream*.

Violet family

Flowering: May - Aug

Marsh Woundwort *Stachys palustris*/Brisgean nan Caorach

Habitat: locally frequent in ditches and damp grassland, including roadsides on Tiree.

A tall, late summer flowering plant with attractive lilac-pink flowers in **whorled spikes**. Each flower has a **hood** and a patterned lower **lip** for enticing insects to the nectar inside the flower **tube**. The tough, erect stem is square in shape, with ridges at the corners; whilst the **opposite** pairs of leaves occur in a widely separated alternate spiral up the stem. The upper leaves have no stalks. The similar, but now rare, Common Hemp-nettle has pinker flowers, more leaves and a distinctively bristly **calyx** with pointed teeth. Purple-loosestrife (page 20) occurs in similar places to Marsh Woundwort, but its flowers are a much deeper purple and bear five petals of equal length.

Form:	**erect**, up to 80cm, (can reach 100cm).
Flowers:	up to 15mm long.
Leaves:	**opposite, tear-drop shaped**, up to 12cm long.

Since the time of the Ancient Greeks, Woundwort has been used in poultices to stop bleeding. The plant most likely to be seen on Coll is, in fact, a hybrid of Marsh and Hedge Woundwort. Hedge Woundwort is a rare plant on both islands, and Marsh Woundwort has not been officially recorded on Coll since 1994.

Dead-nettle family

Flowering: Jul - Sep   Leaves only: Jun

27

Early-purple Orchid *Orchis mascula*/Moth-urach

Habitat: local but frequent in coastal grassland.

The ten to fifty pinkish-purple flowers form a loose **raceme** and give off a honey-like scent when fresh, but smell distinctly like cat urine when older. This early-flowering species has erect **lateral sepals**, like angel's wings. The **dorsal sepals** and **dorsal petals** form a loose **hood**, and all are usually unmarked. The dark-spotted **lip** is broad and three-lobed. The two outer lobes are slightly folded back, and the central lobe is notched and often paler. All three lobes appear slightly crinkled. The **spur** is blunt and upturned. The green stem is usually purplish towards the top, is sheathed with two to three pointed stem leaves, and has four to eight glossy **basal** leaves, which may be dark spotted. This orchid can be confused with darker specimens of Northern Marsh-orchid (opposite). The **lip**, **spur** and leaves give the best clues for identification.

Form:	**erect**, 10cm-40cm, (can reach 60cm).
Flowers:	loose **raceme**, 5cm-15cm long.
Leaves:	**basal**, oblong; stem leaves, spiral, sheathing.

This species is fairly common in woodlands elsewhere in Britain, but retreats to coastal cliffs on the islands, where it is safe from grazing.

  Orchid family

Flowering: Apr - Jun

Northern Marsh-orchid *Dactylorhiza purpurella/*
Mogairlean Purpaidh

Habitat: local in damp pastures and roadside verges on Coll, though less frequent on Tiree.

The ten to forty, bright magenta-purple flowers form a dense square-topped **spike.** This is the only deep magenta-purple orchid to be found on these islands, although some darker specimens might be confused with Early-purple Orchid (opposite). Northern Marsh-orchid's **lateral sepals** are erect, like rabbit's ears; the **dorsal sepals** and **dorsal petals** form a loose **hood**, and all are usually unmarked. The **lip** is diamond shaped, hardly lobed at all, and heavily marked with a series of concentric rings, lines and/or dots. Like all marsh-orchids, the **spur** is broad and conical. The blue-green, broadly **oval basal** leaves sheath the stem and are usually unspotted. The stem leaves are narrow and more pointed.

Form:	**erect**, 10cm-35cm.
Flowers:	**spike**, 5cm-6cm long, 3cm-4cm across.
Leaves:	**oval**.

This is one of the most abundant orchids in the north and west of Scotland and often grows on roadside verges. The hybrid Northern Marsh-orchid x Common Spotted-orchid might be encountered on both islands.

Orchid family

Purple Milk-vetch *Astragalus danicus*/Bliachd-pheasair Charcra

Habitat: a rare plant, found only on steep, south-facing, grassy slopes on Ceann a' Mhara, Tiree.

The attractive, pea-shaped flowers are clustered on erect stalks and are deep violet with dark purple veins and a whiter central area. The ladder-like leaves end in a leaflet, not a **tendril**. Bush Vetch (page 39) is superficially similar, but the flowers lack the central white area and are arranged in clusters, and the leaflets are much broader. The dark-brown fruit **pod** of Purple Milk-vetch is swollen and covered in dense, white hairs.

Form:	**erect**, less than 12cm, (can reach 30cm).
Flowers:	up to 18mm long.
Leaves:	**pinnate** with paired, **oval** leaflets up to 15mm long.
Fruit:	**pod**, up to 8mm.

This is a rare and declining plant in Britain due to lack of grazing, and grassland 'improvement'. The colony on Tiree is the most western in Great Britain. Other colonies are also found on the Aran Islands in Co. Clare, Ireland.

Pea family

Flowering: Jun - Jul   Seeds: Jul - Aug

Harebell *Campanula rotundifolia*/Currag Cuthaige

Habitat: common on dunes and rock ledges on Coll, more local in similar places on Tiree.

A beautiful, delicate plant with sky-blue, bell-shaped flowers with sharp triangular teeth. The flowers form a loose cluster at the end of slender, hairless stalks and are often seen nodding in the breeze. The long, narrow upper leaves hug the stem. The rotund **basal** leaves have small, white dots on their edges, are long stalked and usually wither away before before the plant flowers.

Form:	**erect**, 20cm-40cm, (can reach 50cm).
Flowers:	12mm-20mm long.
Leaves:	**basal**, rounded; stem leaves, **linear**.

Often known as Scottish Bluebell, the beauty of the plant is celebrated in the traditional song *The Bluebell of Scotland*: "The heath bell, the harebell, Old Scotland's bell of blue". (Bluebell is a separate species, page 32). In the Outer Hebrides children used to eat the flower heads, and cuckoos wear them on their heads! The Gaelic translates as 'cuckoo's cap'.

Bellflower family

Flowering: Jul - Sep   Leaves only: Jun

Bluebell *Hyacinthoides non-scripta*/Bròg na Cuthaig

Habitat: occasional on rock ledges and ruins on Tiree, more frequent and widespread on rocks and amongst bracken on Coll.

Form: erect, up to 30cm (can reach 50cm).

Flowers: 14mm-20mm long.

Leaves: basal, linear, up to 30cm long and 20mm wide.

Fruit: oval.

The Bluebell is a familiar and attractive plant with nodding, stalked flowers clustered towards the top of the stem. The sweet-smelling flowers are small, bell shaped and violet-blue. They bear creamy-white **anthers** and petals that curl distinctively at their tips. The slender, glossy, dark green leaves turn yellow-green with age. The plant is rather localised on Tiree, being easiest to see on the cliff ledges at Ceann a' Mhara, but is more widespread on Coll, particularly in the rocky eastern half of the island, where it also carpets the small offshore islands. It can be seen growing amongst trees at The Lodge on Coll and is typical of mainland woods.

The Bluebell occasionally occurs with pink or white flowers. In some parts of Scotland, Bluebell is also the name for the Harebell (page 31). The Gaelic name translates as 'shoe of the cuckoo'.

 Lily family

Flowering: Apr - Jun   Leaves only: Mar   Seeds: Jul-Aug

Spring Squill *Scilla verna*/Lear-uinnean

Habitat: widespread but local on cliff-top turf and rocky ledges on Tiree and Coll.

Dense patches of these pale blue flowers rising from short turf are one of the delights of spring. The fine, yellow-green grass-like leaves appear from **perennial** bulbs in late March and persist until the autumn, when they turn orange at the tips. Each flower consists of six flattened petals with green **bracts** arranged around the protruding blue **anthers** and **style**. These are clustered at

the top of the stem. The small seeds are held in small, grey-brown cases.

Spring Squill flowers in advance of most other species and provides an early source of nectar for solitary bees. The plant was widely known as 'Sea Onion', which is a direct translation of the Gaelic, and its bulbs have long been known as a source of medicine, valued for its expectorant and diuretic properties.

Form: **erect**, up to 12cm (can reach 15cm).

Flowers: up to 15mm across.

Leaves: **basal, linear**, up to 15cm long.

Fruit: small, grey-brown seed cases.

Lily family

Devil's-bit Scabious *Succisa pratensis*/Ura-bhallach

Habitat: locally abundant in damp grassland and marshes.

Devil's-bit Scabious has an upright stem holding a dense **flower-head** of mauve to dark purplish-blue flowers with protruding **stamens**. It is a characteristic flower of late summer in damp machair. Here it can grow in profusion with vast colonies of the softly luminous Grass-of-Parnassus (page 145), creating a magical colour scheme, particularly noticeable on Coll. The flowers can occasionally be pink or white. The **basal** leaves have a noticeable whitish mid-rib and both **basal** and stem leaves are undivided.

Form: erect up to 35cm, (can reach 1m).

Flowers: flower-heads, 1cm-2cm wide.

Leaves: basal leaves, mainly **oval**, 3cm-5cm long; stem leaves, narrower and **opposite**.

The legend of its name is widespread through Europe and tells how the Devil found the plant in paradise but, envying its beneficial properties to mankind, bit the root in half. Devil's-bit Scabious can be used as a tea for coughs or fevers, as an ointment for skin complaints, and as a hair wash for dandruff. The powdered root can be used to expel internal worms.

Teasel family

Flowering: Jul - Oct

Water Mint *Mentha aquatica*/Meannt an Arbhair

Habitat: widespread and frequent in wet places such as ditches, pool-edges and marshes.

This plant has a characteristic sickly-sweet, minty smell, particularly when the leaves are crushed. It is the only common mint on the islands. This a well-known wetland plant, with one or two large **whorls** of pinkish-lilac flowers bunched at the top of the stout, hairy stem, often with a third, more separate, **whorl** lower down. The long **stamens** project out of the flowers, giving them a fluffy appearance. The leaves are hairy and the lower leaves have short stalks and often show a purplish tinge.

Form: erect, up to 30cm (can reach 90cm).

Flowers: up to 5mm long.

Leaves: opposite, **tear-drop shaped**, **toothed**, up to 8cm long.

In the Outer Hebrides, a poultice of crushed Water Mint used to be applied as a cure for athlete's foot. Today, Water Mint is one of many plants that are used to assist in purifying the water in reedbed waste-removal systems.

Dead-nettle family

Flowering: Jul - Sep

35

Oysterplant *Mertensia maritima*/Tiodhlac na Mara

Habitat: rare, occurs only on loose shingle near the top of sheltered beaches. Currently one large population at a single site in north Tiree, and a few scattered plants on SW Coll.

An unusual low-growing plant of coarse sand and shingle. The small, deep blue flowers are clustered at the end of the trailing stems, and are initially pinkish, slowly turning a deep purple-blue. The distinctive grey-green leaves are rubbery and rough in texture, with a hard point at the tip and a pronounced central vein. The thick fleshy stems become tinged purple with age.

Form: **trailing**, up to 60cm long.

Flowers: up to 6mm long and 15mm across.

Leaves: **oval** to **tear-drop shaped**, up to 8cm long.

A scarce plant that is sporadic in occurrence and generally declining in numbers. Colonies can persist for many years, but are slowly out-competed by other salt-tolerant plants from stable shingle. The plant requires storms from time to time to provide fresh shingle habitat to exploit. The rubbery leaves are edible and taste a little like oysters! The Gaelic translates as 'gift of the sea'.

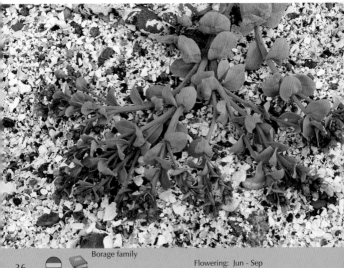

Borage family

Flowering: Jun - Sep

Selfheal *Prunella vulgaris*/Dubhan Ceann-chòsach

Habitat: very common in grasslands.

Selfheal's **flower-head** is dense and oblong, consisting of many purplish, lobed, **tubed** flowers. The complex **flower-head** takes a little getting used to and is worth a closer look. Each of the tubular flowers can mature at different times, giving it a somewhat ragged appearance. When all the purple flowers eventually fall, the remaining brownish **bracts** can look like a completely different plant. Each individual flower is pollinated separately by bees.

Form: **sprawling** to **erect**, up to 10cm (can reach 30cm).

Flowers: up to 1cm long.

Leaves: **oval** to **triangular**, sparsely hairy, sometimes **toothed**, 1cm-3cm long.

Unsurprisingly for a plant named Selfheal, there are many published remedies, both ancient and modern: "There is not a better Wound herb in the world"; "A salve will heal any green wound (gangrene)"; "The juice used with oil of roses to anoint the temples is very effectual to remove the headache"; "Mixed with the honey of roses it cleaneth and healeth ulcers in the mouth and throat" (Grieve 1931). The literal translation of the Gaelic is 'spongy kidney head', perhaps in reference to yet another healing property, "it removes all obstructions of the liver, spleen and kidneys." (Clyne 1989).

Flowering: Jun - Oct

Dead-nettle family

37

Field Gentian *Gentianella campestris*/Lus a' Chrùbain

Habitat: occasional in short, dry grassland on rock outcrops, often near fixed dunes on Coll.

Field Gentian has small clusters of flowers growing up and at the top of its slightly branching stem. The flowers are blue-lilac (rarely white) and are bell shaped with a fringe of hairs at the mouth of the petal **tube**. Gentians form a numerous group with almost two hundred species worldwide, although it is currently thought that Field Gentian is the only one found on Tiree and Coll. Field Gentian can be identified by the two wide **sepals** overlapping the two narrow inner ones. When sitting on a grassy knoll admiring the sea views, look around you: gentians like those places too.

Form: **erect**, 3cm-10cm tall, (can reach up to 30cm).

Flowers: up to 2cm long.

Leaves: **basal** leaves **oval** and blunt; stem leaves more pointed, up to 2cm long.

The name Gentian derives from Gentius, King of Illyria (180-167 BC), who apparently discovered the plant's medicinal value. Gentians are intensely bitter and are valuable tonics. They were used in the Middle Ages to treat undernourished cattle that were reluctant to come into season, and more recently for human digestive problems, including poisoning and kidney stones.

Gentian family

Flowering: Jul - Sep

Bush Vetch *Vicia sepium*/Peasair nam Preas
Tufted Vetch *Vicia cracca*/Peasair nan Luch

Habitat: Bush Vetch is occasional, but widespread, in grassland including rocky areas, dunes and fields.

Tufted Vetch is common on machair, dunes and along roadsides.

Bush Vetch

Form: **climbing**, up to 50cm (can reach 60cm).

Flowers: 12mm-15mm across.

Leaves: **alternate**, **pinnate** with 5-9 pairs of bluntly **oval** leaflets up to 3cm long.

These two vetches have very different flowers. Bush Vetch has tight clusters of a smaller number of larger, pinkish-purple flowers, bearing darker veins, whilst the numerous smaller flowers of Tufted Vetch are a deep violet-blue and are arranged in **racemes**, with each flower on a tiny stalk of equal length. The flowers of Bush Vetch quickly turn brown after being pollinated and form black seed **pods**, whereas Tufted Vetch has brown seed **pods**. Tufted Vetch is often a larger plant and has more numerous, hairier and longer leaflets than Bush Vetch. Both species have branched, twisting **tendrils** at the end of each leaf, with which they climb up through other vegetation.

Tufted Vetch

Form: **climbing**, up to 100cm (can reach 200cm).

Flowers: 8mm-12mm across.

Leaves: **alternate**, **pinnate** with 6-15 pairs of narrowly **oval** leaflets up to 5cm long.

Pea family

Flowering: Jun - Oct

Common Dog-violet *Viola riviniana*/Dail-chuach Coitcheann

Habitat: Common Dog-violet is common and widespread on heath, cliffs and machair.

Common Dog-violet shows considerable variation in the blue-purple tone of its flowers. It has five petals, usually overlapping, pointed **sepals** and a blunt, pale **spur** (never darker then the petals) that is notched at the tip. On the heath and dunes you will also see Heath Dog-violet which is paler and bluer. Although it also has five petals, they don't overlap, and it has a short greenish-yellow **spur**. The leaves of Common Dog-violet are **heart shaped** and long stalked, whereas those of Heath Dog-violet are more **oval** and are thick and fleshy.

Form:	**erect,** up to 20cm.
Flowers:	12mm-20mm across, 5 petals, usually overlapping.
Leaves:	**basal**, non-flowering **rosette**, **heart shaped**, 15mm-20mm, as broad as long.

Common Dog-violet starts flowering earlier and often flowers twice through the season, so is often in flower before and well after Heath Dog-violet which only flowers in May and June. Heath Dog-violet is listed as 'near threatened' in *The Vascular Plant Red Data List for Great Britain*.

Violet family

Flowering: Apr - Aug

Common Butterwort *Pinguicula vulgaris*/Mòthan

Habitat: common on wet heath and poor damp grassland.

Butterworts are carnivorous plants, which use their sticky leaves to trap and then digest midges, amongst other insects. They are distinctive plants with a **rosette** of spreading, oblong to **oval**, yellow-green leaves that looks like a starfish. The leaf edges roll inwards and the tip is pointed. From the **rosette** arise stems with solitary violet or purple flowers. The five petals form a lobed **tube** which is open at mouth with a white throat patch. There is a back-pointing **spur** which tapers to a point. See also Pale Butterwort (page 77).

Common Butterwort is an important plant in Hebridean herbalism and in folklore. It can be used to curdle milk for butter or cheese and the sticky leaves can be applied to sore and chapped hands. Butterwort is considered to be a plant of good fortune. A person who had a miraculous escape had "drunk the milk of the cow that ate the Mòthan" (Milliken & Bridgewater 2004).

Form:	**erect**, 5cm-15cm.
Flowers:	14mm-22mm.
Leaves:	**basal rosette,** oblong to **oval**, pointed at tip, 2cm-8cm long.

Bladderwort family

Germander Speedwell *Veronica chamaedrys*/Nuallach
Marsh Speedwell *Veronica scutellata*/Lus-crè Lèana
Blue Water-speedwell *Veronica anagallis-aquatica*/Fualachda
Wall Speedwell *Veronica arvensis*/Lus-crè Balla

Habitat: Germander Speedwell and Wall Speedwell are common in dry grasslands, while Marsh Speedwell and Blue Water-Speedwell are occasional in wetland and stream habitats.

Germander Speedwell

Form: **erect**, 5cm-15cm, (can reach 50cm).

Flowers: 1cm across.

Leaves: **tear-drop** shaped, 10mm-25mm long, coarsely and bluntly **toothed**.

Speedwells are herbs with **opposite** leaves and flat, four-petalled flowers. The lower petal is smaller, and there are four **sepals** and two protruding **stamens**. Aside from these four speedwells growing in different habitats and with different forms, identification of each species requires a careful look at flowers, leaves and stem hairs. Germander and Wall Speedwell have similar shaped leaves which are **toothed** to varying degrees. Wall Speedwell, however has lower leaves that have short stalks and upper leaves with no stalks. All of Germander's leaves have no stalks and it has two distinctive opposite rows of long, white hairs on the stem, while Wall Speedwell has a generally downy stem. Wall Speedwell has flower stalks that are shorter than its **bracts**, while those of Germander are long-stalked, on a flowering **raceme** that arises from one or both junctions of the upper leaf pairs. The **raceme** of Wall Speedwell is long and terminal.

The stalkless leaves of Marsh and Blue Water-speedwell are similar in shape, but those of Blue Water are slightly **toothed**. The flower stalk of Marsh Speedwell is twice the length of its **bract**, and flower **racemes** will arise from only one junction of any given leaf pair and stem. In contrast, Blue Water-speedwell has flower stalks that are equal to or longer than its **bracts** and has flower **racemes** arising from both junctions of any given leaf pair and stem. The flowers of both can be pale blue, but Marsh Speedwell has purple lines on its petals and can also be white or pink. Both have hairless stems.

The petals are lightly attached, so any jarring causes the bright blossom to drop – hence, perhaps, the name speedwell and other local names such as 'farewell' and 'goodbye'. In some areas it can be called 'Angels' eyes' or 'Eye of Christ', because of the beautiful intense blue of the flowers. There are about twenty species in the UK. Writers of old from many countries speak highly of the virtues of speedwell as a remedy for various skin diseases. Gerard, the early Herbalist, recommends it for cancer, "given in good broth of a hen." (Grieve 1931).

Marsh Speedwell

Form:	**creeping** to **erect**, up to 25cm, (can reach 60cm).
Flowers:	6mm-7mm across.
Leaves:	**lance shaped**, 2cm-4cm long, **untoothed**.

Blue Water-speedwell

Form:	**creeping** to **erect**, up to 25cm, (can reach 50cm).
Flowers:	5mm-6mm across.
Leaves:	**lance shaped**, 2cm-4cm long, scarcely **toothed**.

Wall Speedwell

Form:	**erect**, 5cm-15cm, (can reach 30cm).
Flowers:	4mm-5mm across.
Leaves:	**oval**-triangular, up to 15mm long, coarsely **toothed**.

Heather *Calluna vulgaris*/Fraoch
Bell Heather *Erica cinerea*/Fraoch a' Bhadain
Cross-leaved Heath *Erica tetralix*/Fraoch Frangach

Habitat: Heather is common and widespread on heath, preferring dry areas. Bell Heather is frequent and widespread on dry heath and rocks, preferring dry areas. Cross-leaved Heath is common and widespread on heath, preferring wetter areas.

These three common evergreen shrubs are superficially similar, but have several subtle differences. The flowers are different in size and colour, and their habitats differ. Heather and Bell Heather tend to grow together in areas of dry heath, with Heather the dominant plant. Cross-leaved Heath has a strong preference for wet conditions, often growing in old, hill ditches and abandoned peat cuttings as well as bogs. Heather's small, bell-shaped flowers appear in **spikes** and are pale pink-purple (very occasionally white). Bell Heather also has bell-shaped flowers, but they are larger, generally more purplish in tone and are arranged in short **racemes**. Cross-leaved Heath's flowers are globular and appear in compact, terminal, one-sided clusters. They are the pinkest and largest flowers. The leaves are all similar, but Cross-leaved Heath has leaves that form a distinctive cross when viewed from above. Additionally, it is hairy, with greyish, rather than dark, green leaves.

Heather		
Form:	erect and carpeting, up to 60cm, (can reach 150cm).	
Flowers:	3mm-5mm long.	
Leaves:	4 columns, **linear**, 1mm-2mm.	

Crowberry family

Bell Heather

Form: **erect**, up to 50cm, (can reach 60cm).

Flowers: 4mm-6mm long.

Leaves: **whorls** of 3, **linear**, 3mm-6mm.

Cross-leaved Heath

Form: **erect**, up to 60cm, (can reach 70cm).

Flowers: 5mm-9mm long.

Leaves: **whorls** of 4, **linear**, hairy, 2mm-5mm.

Flowering: Heather: Jul - Sep
Bell Heather & Cross-leaved Heath: Jun - Sep

Cross-leaved

Common Milkwort *Polygala vulgaris*/Lus a' Bhainne

Habitat: widespread and common in short grassland.

Common Milkwort has up to twenty small, usually blue flowers, on short stalks, towards the top of the stem. The flowers can be purple, pink or white. The petals are joined together to make a little whitish, fringed tube. Common Milkwort has **alternate** leaves, while the very similar Heath Milkwort has **opposite** lower leaves. Both milkworts have pointed, **oval** lower leaves, which become narrower and more **lance shaped** further up the stem. Common Milkwort is usually found in grassy areas on more alkaline soils, whilst the Heath Milkwort, not surprisingly, grows in heathy areas on more acid soils.

Form: **erect**, 5cm-20cm, (can reach 30cm).

Flowers: 6mm-10mm long.

Leaves: **alternate**, **oval** to **lance shaped**, up to 35mm.

Milkwort has been thought to increase the milk yields from cows grazed on pastures where it is plentiful. The Latin name Polygala means 'much milk', probably alluding to the plant's secretions, and their effects.

Milkwort family

Flowering: May - Sep

Water Lobelia *Lobelia dortmanna*/Flùr an Lochain

Habitat: frequent in acidic lochs with gravely bottoms and particularly common in the NE lochs of Coll.

This delicate and handsome aquatic flower grows on slender, leafless, hollow stems. The **basal rosette** of fleshy, **linear** leaves is submerged. Along the stems grow the nodding, stalked, white or pale mauve flowers, made up of a two-lipped **corolla**, formed by three downward-pointing and two upward-pointing petal-lobes.

Form: erect, 40cm-70cm, (can reach 120cm).

Flowers: 40cm-70cm, (can reach 120cm).

Leaves: rosette, linear, 2cm-4cm long

This plant is characteristic of oligotrophic lochs (nutrient-poor with clear water); it will die out if the water becomes rich in nutrients, which can come from agricultural run-off. Damselflies love to perch on Water Lobelia.

Bellflower family

Wild Thyme *Thymus polytrichus*/Lus an Righ

Habitat: very common in short, dry grassland.

Wild Thyme is a lovely little plant, found throughout the islands, but often overlooked as it is so small. Sit anywhere in a dry, grassy, flower-filled area and look closely at the turf. Look for the tiny, pale purple flowers (sometimes appearing as pink), and their creeping mat of dark green, flat, paired leaves. When the plant is in flower, the leaves are faintly thyme-scented when crushed. Before flowering, the leaves exude their smell without being crushed. The stems are square and very hairy on two sides. The tiny flowers form a rounded head.

Form: **creeping**, and mat forming, up to 5cm, (can reach 10cm).

Flowers: 5mm-6mm long.

Leaves: **opposite**, **oval**, up to 7mm.

The Gaelic translates as 'plant of the King'. An old tradition says that Wild Thyme fragranced the bed of the Virgin Mary. Shakespeare must have been dreaming of the machair when he supposed that the abode of the Faerie Queen was "the bank whereon the wild thyme blows" (Shakespeare 1595). Bees are especially fond of Wild Thyme, which gives a particular taste to the local honey. It is still widely used as a condiment, or as a tea.

Dead-nettle family

Flowering: Jun - Sep

Bugloss *Anchusa arvensis*/Lus Teangaan Daimh

Habitat: occasional on bare, sandy, or cultivated areas in grassland. Widespread on Tiree, in patches of disturbed ground.

Bugloss is an annual that springs up when bare, sandy ground is exposed in fields or dunes. It is distinctive for the combination of small, pretty blue flowers on a big, bristly plant. The **inflorescence** is often forked, with the flowers borne in clusters. Each flower has a white centre, a curved **tube** at its base and leafy **bracts**. The flowers can resemble those of the Forget-me-not (page 50), or speedwells (pages 42,43), but the big, bristling nature of Bugloss is distinctive. The upper leaves clasp the stem and have **heart-shaped** bases, while the lower leaves are stalked. All are bristly and wavy edged and generally **lance shaped** to oblong.

Form: **erect**, up to 40cm (can reach 50cm).

Flowers: 40mm-6mm across.

Leaves: **alternate**, **lance shaped** to oblong, up to 10cm long.

The name Bugloss derives from the Greek for ox tongue, which the leaves are said to resemble in both shape and texture. The Gaelic translates as 'stag's tongue'.

Borage family

Field Forget-me-not *Myosotis arvensis*/Lus Midhe Tràth
Tufted Forget-me-not *Myosotis laxa*/Lus Midhe Dosach

Habitat: Field Forget-me-not is locally common in cultivated fields. Tufted Forget-me-not is widespread in marshy places.

Field Forget-me-not

Forget-me-nots are beautiful and well-known flowers. They have delicate clusters of sky blue flowers with a yellow centre, and are often pink in bud. These two species can be differentiated by several means: Field Forget-me-not occurs in dry habitats; Tufted Forget-me-not in wet. On close examination Tufted Forget-me-not has the hairs on the stem closely pressed in and it has straight hairs on its **sepal**. By comparison, the stem hairs of Field Forget-me-not spread out and its **sepal** hairs are hooked. The leaves of both are similar in shape, though Field Forget-me-not leaves tend to be slightly more pointed and its lower leaves are stalked. The upper leaves of Field Forget-me-not and all of the leaves of Tufted Forget-me-not have no stalks. You will also see Water Forget-me-not in burns and other wet places. It has creeping runners which Tufted Forget-me-not lacks.

Form: **erect**, up to 30cm, (Field can reach 40cm; Tufted can reach 50cm).

Flowers: 2mm-5mm across.

Leaves: oblong to **oval shaped**.

This is a flower that speaks of love and separation. Giving the flower to an absent lover to keep love strong also reflects folk lore that the juice of the plant hardens steel.

Tufted Forget-me-not

Field   Borage family

Tufted

Flowering: May - Aug

Introduction to the red-pink section

This section starts very boldly with the large flowers of the Long-headed Poppy and Sea Bindweed. Just as spectacular, if you care to get down on your hands and knees, are the tiny, delicate flowers of Bog Pimpernel or Sea-milkwort. Enjoying these islands is partly about appreciating things on a small scale. We do not have the Grand Canyon, but we do have magnificent sand sculptures on our beaches and in the dunes, which evolve and change with the wind and tides. Look closely at the ground and you will start to appreciate the intricate mix of flora and fauna. As with the comments preceding the blue-purple section, please be aware that the decision to name a flower pink or purple can be subjective, or can depend on seasonal variations. Marsh Lousewort, for example, has pink-purple flowers. In order to best distinguish it from the other Lousewort, it appears on a composite page in this section. Sea Rocket normally has white flowers, but they can appear as lilac pink. The sundews have inconspicuous white flowers, and are quite noticeable for the red-tipped hairs on the leaves. Although red is the eye-catching colour, they appear in the white section for their flower colour. If you do not find what you seek, check in a closely related colour section!

Red Clover

Long-headed Poppy *Papaver dubium* subsp. *dubium/*

Habitat: very local in cultivated ground.

Although similar to the familiar Common Poppy, the four, papery, pinky-red petals of Long-headed Poppy are smaller, not quite so crimson and lack the dark basal blotch. The flower grows on a thin, hairy stem to which the fine hairs press closely. The long, smooth, club-shaped brown seed **capsule** is the main distinguishing feature, this being the only red poppy showing such a long, hairless head. The leaves of the **basal rosette** are **glaucous**.

Form:	**erect,** 20cm-60cm.
Flowers:	3cm-7cm across.
Leaves:	**basal rosette**, **pinnate** with lobed leaflets; stem leaves, small.
Fruit:	narrow, elongated, length more than 1.5 times width.

Poppy seeds have been used as an adornment to bread since Roman times. The juice of the flowers has been used as a mild sedative and, in the Uists, as an ingredient in liquid teething mixtures for toddlers. The seeds can remain viable in soil for a very long time. Seeds recovered from excavations and dated at fifty years old are reported to have germinated. All parts of the plant are mildly poisonous, and the sap may cause skin irritation.

Poppy family

Flowering: Jun - Aug   Seeds: Jul - Aug

Sea Bindweed *Calystegia soldanella*/Flur a' Phrionnsa

Habitat: rare and very local in dunes and on pebbly ground at the top of beaches.

Sea Bindweed has large attractive trumpet-like flowers in which the petals are fused together at the base. These are largely pink and bear five white lines radiating from the centre, whereas those of the similar Large Bindweed (page 137) are entirely white. The tough twisting stems wind around objects close to the ground and are often partly buried, whilst they lack the **tendrils** of other bindweeds. The leaves are notched at the base, and are small, **kidney shaped** and fleshy.

Form:	**trailing**/weakly climbing, up to 60cm, (can reach 100cm).
Flowers:	30mm-55mm across.
Leaves:	**kidney shaped**, up to 3cm long.

The fleshy leaves help the plant to retain moisture in the rather well-drained sites that it inhabits. The flexible stems were formerly used as string for tying, which was regarded as strong but not long-lasting.

Bindweed family

Flowering: Jul - Sep   Leaves only: Jun

53

Great Willowherb *Epilobium hirsutum*/Seileachan Mòr
Rosebay Willowherb *Chamerion angustifolium*/Seileachan Franga

Habitat: Great Willowherb is occasional in roadside ditches and other wet places in West Tiree only, not on Coll. Rosebay Willowherb occurs at two sites in West Tiree, and several places at the north of Coll.

Great Willowherb

Form: **erect**, up to 180cm.

Flowers: 10mm-16mm across.

Leaves: **opposite, lance shaped**, up to 15cm long.

The leaves of both Rosebay and Great Willowherb can be used to make tea. Rosebay Willowherb thrives in areas that have been burnt, including bombsites - hence its alternative name, 'Fireweed'.

Both of the large willowherbs on the islands have attractive pink flowers, but are easily distinguished from one another (Also see Marsh and Hoary Willowherb, page 72). Great Willowherb is restricted to West Tiree, and its loose display of large, saucer-shaped flowers bear creamy white central **stamens**. Rosebay Willowherb grows in drier places; its many, stalked flowers form a distinct pyramid and mature slowly from the bottom to the tip. All willowherb leaves are long and pointed, but those of Rosebay Willowherb have rather wavy edges.

Rosebay Willowherb

Form: **erect**, up to 150cm.

Flowers: 20mm-30mm across.

Leaves: **alternate, lance shaped**, up to 30cm lor

 Great   Willowherb family

 Rosebay   Flowering: Jul - Sep

Common Spotted-orchid *Dactylorhiza fuchsii*/Urach Bhallach

Habitat: abundant in moist, base-rich grasslands.

The Common Spotted-orchid has a closely packed pyramidal/cylindrical **spike** of twenty to seventy pale lilac/pink flowers. This species is extremely variable, but generally the flowers have **lateral sepals** spread like wings, and a loose **hood** formed by **dorsal sepals** and **dorsal petals**, all of which is marked with purplish lines and dots on a pale lilac/pinkish background. The **lip** has three well defined lobes. The two outer lobes are rhombic. The central lobe is longer, triangular, and is marked with a symmetrical double loop, inside which is a series of lines and/or

dots. The **spur** is straight and slender, unlike the broad, conical **spur** of the marsh-orchids (pages 29 & 56) The green, grooved stem is often purplish towards the top, and the leaves are usually spotted, blotched or barred brownish-purple.

Form:	**erect** 7cm-50cm, (can reach 70cm).
Flowers:	**spike**, up to 15cm long.
Leaves:	**basal**, broadly **lance shaped**; stem leaves **lance shaped** becoming narrower towards the **spike**.

The hybrids Common Spotted-orchid x Heath Spotted-orchid and Common Spotted-orchid x Northern Marsh-orchid might be encountered on both islands. Research is underway on orchid hybrids and subspecies. The photo shown is actually of a hybrid, but it clearly shows the key features of the species and is typical of many of the orchids you will see on the islands

Orchid family

Early Marsh-orchid *Dactylorhiza incarnata/Mogairlean Lèana*

Habitat: frequent in damp meadows, wet machair and dune slacks.

This species comes in two forms on Coll and Tiree: *Dactylorhiza incarnata* subsp. *incarnata* and *Dactylorhiza incarnata* subsp. *coccinea*. Although subsp. *incarnata* is the usual form found throughout Britain, the subsp. *coccinea* is by far the commonest form on these islands.

The **lateral sepals** of *Dactylorhiza incarnata* subsp. *incarnata* are erect, like rabbit's ears, with the **dorsal sepals** and **dorsal petals** forming a tight **hood**, all marked with loops and dots on a pale pinkish background. The **lip** has three lobes, the outer two being folded back, giving the impression of a thin flower. The **lip** is marked with a reddish double loop, inside which are a series of lines and/or dots. Like all marsh-orchids, the **spur** is broad and conical. The stem is apple-green.

Dactylorhiza incarnata subsp. *coccinea* is short and stocky, often appearing stemless, with broad-based tapering leaves and flowers that are an unmistakable stunning, deep red colour. It frequently grows in swarms of over one hundred plants on the machair, occasionally side by side with a few subsp. *incarnata*. Both subspecies have three to six, unspotted, apple-green **basal** leaves that sheath the stem. The fifteen to thirty flowers which form a dense pyramidal spike are either pale pink or deep red.

Form: **erect**, 10cm-25cm, (can reach 30cm).

Flowers: spike, 5cm-10cm.

Leaves: basal, pointedly **oval**, stem: narrow and pointed

Below left: subsp. *coccinea*   Below right: subsp. *incarnata*

Orchid family

Flowering: May - Jul

Heath Fragrant-orchid *Gymnadenia borealis*/Lus Taghte

Habitat: local on base-rich grassland on Coll, but only one old record from Tiree.

This delicate-looking orchid is the commonest of the fragrant-orchids in Scotland. It has twenty to thirty pinkish-purple unmarked flowers in a long, slim, cylindrical **spike**, and gives off a sweet scent, recalling cloves. Individual flowers have small, oval **lateral sepals**, held at a slight downwards angle and pressed backwards. The **dorsal sepals** and **dorsal petals** form a loose **hood**. The **lip** is longer than wide, has two small side lobes and a longer central lobe. The **spur** is long and slender, and more purplish in colour. The green stem is usually purplish-brown towards the top, with three to five unmarked **basal** leaves and two to three narrower stem leaves.

Form: **erect**, 10cm-250cm.

Flowers: spike, 6cm-15cm long.

Leaves: basal, **linear** to **lance shaped**; stem leaves, **lance shaped.**

Until recently, Fragrant Orchid was considered to be a single species with three distinct forms, but taxonomists have now decided that there are actually three different species. The much more robust and taller Marsh Fragrant-orchid *Gymnadenia densiflora*, which can have up to one hundred flowers in a spike, has occasionally been recorded on Coll.

Orchid family

Flowering: Jun - Jul

Habitat: common (locally abundant) on acid grassland and heath.

The five to twenty pale pink/mauve flowers form a compact, pyramidal **spike**, which is faintly scented. It usually grows in clumps, often with up to one hundred specimens. The **lateral sepals** are spread like wings; the **dorsal sepals** and **dorsal petals** form a loose **hood**. The **lip** is broad and skirt-like, with a short and triangular central lobe. The whole flower is marked with a series of reddish/purple lines, circles and dots, rarely showing the symmetrical double loop characteristic of Common Spotted-orchid (page 55). The **spur** is straight and slender, unlike the broad conical **spur** of the marsh-orchids (page 29 & 56). The green, slightly ridged stem is sheathed by the variably spotted **basal** leaves and is often washed purple towards the **spike**.

Form:	erect, 10cm-25cm, (can reach 40cm).
Flowers:	**spike**, 10cm long.
Leaves:	**lance shaped**.

This species is prone to sun bleaching and can often appear almost entirely white. The hybrids Heath Spotted-orchid x Common Spotted-orchid and Heath Spotted-orchid x Northern Marsh-orchid might be encountered on both islands.

Orchid family

Flowering: May - Aug   Leaves only: May

Pyramidal Orchid *Anacamptis pyramidalis*/Mogairlean nan Coilleag

Habitat: common and widespread on dunes and machair of SW Coll. Very local, although quite numerous on Tiree.

Form:	**erect**, 10cm-60cm.
Flowers:	**spike**, 2cm-5cm.
Leaves:	**basal rosette** and spiral up stem, **lance shaped**.

The fifty to one hundred tightly packed pinkish-purple flowers form a pyramidal **spike**, which becomes more domed with age. This is one of the easiest orchids to identify. The individual flowers have blunt, spreading, **lateral sepals** that are very wing-like, with the **dorsal sepals** and **dorsal petals** forming a tight **hood**. This species has an unmarked, deeply three-lobed **lip**, and the **spur** is long and straight. The green stem often appears quite flimsy and generally has a distinct kink. The flowers have a sickly-sweet scent, particularly in the evenings. The leaves are grey-green.

Orchid family

Wood Burdock *Arctium nemorosum*/Cliadan

Habitat: occasional, but widespread in waste places, such as roadsides and around farms.

This large, robust plant is shade intolerant and grows in areas of disturbed bare soil. The thistle-like reddish or purple flowers protrude from a spiky ball of **bracts**, which form the well-known sticky 'burs'. The stems are thick and branched, whilst the very large, rough, rhubarb-like leaves are present for longer than the flowers and are **basal** and **alternate**.

Form: **erect**, up to 80cm, (can reach 120cm).

Flowers: **flower-head** up to 25mm across.

Leaves: **basal** and **alternate**, **oval** to **heart shaped**, up to 50cm long.

The leaves, juice and roots were all once used in surgery and medicine. The spherical, spiny seeds catch in the fur of passing animals and in clothing, and are dispersed in this way. Children also like to throw the 'burs' at each other in sticky 'snow-ball' fights!

Daisy family
Flowering: Jul - Aug   Leaves only: May - Jun, Oct   Seeds: Sep - Oct

Habitat: occasional dense patches in roadside ditches.

Butterbur is an unusual, introduced **perennial** plant. The pinkish flowers are borne in dense, cone-like **spikes**. The male and female flowers usually occur on separate **spikes**, but on Tiree and Coll - as in most of Britain - all of the flowers are male, and fruiting does not occur. The leaves are small or absent during flowering, developing later in the summer to become massive and umbrella like, often shading out all other vegetation. They are covered in short soft hairs on the under-surface.

Form: **erect**, up to 100cm.

Flowers: 7mm-12mm wide.

Leaves: **basal**, **heart** to **kidney shaped**, hairy, slightly **toothed**, up to 90cm across.

The large leaves were once used for wrapping butter. The absence of female flowers means that all propagation on the islands is vegetative, with the plants developing each year from deep, thick **rhizomes**.   The Gaelic name, Gallan Mòr, translates as 'big stalk' and the place name Gallanach translates as 'abundant in butterburs'.

Daisy family

Amphibious Bistort *Persicaria amphibia*/Glùineach an Uisage

Habitat: local in wet grassland and wetlands.

Amphibious Bistort comes in two distinct forms, aquatic and terrestrial, both having their clusters of pink flowers in compact, cylindrical **spikes**. The aquatic form is characterised by large patches of floating, long-stalked, hairless leaves with a truncate base, from which arise masses of pink **spikes** of flowers. The terrestrial form has short-stalked, narrow, downy leaves, which are rounded at the base. The stems are usually red. Due to its habitat preference, it might be confused with the closely related Redshank (opposite), but Amphibious Bistort has a much heavier and more substantial flower **spike** with a more uniformly pure pink colour and stemmed leaves. Redshank often has a dark blotch on the upperside of the stemless leaves.

Form:	**erect,** 30cm-60cm.
Flowers:	**spikes**, 2cm-4cm long; individual flower, 2mm-3mm across.
Leaves:	aquatic form is narrow, oblong almost **heart shaped** and hairless; land form is shorter and slightly hairy.
Fruit:	nut like.

Strangely, both the terrestrial and aquatic forms can occur on a single plant in water edge habitats. The root contains high levels of tannin, which was used to cure leather. A yellow dye was also prepared from the roots.

Knotweed family

Flowering: Jun - Sep

Redshank *Persicaria maculosa*/Glùineach Dhearg

Habitat: common in wet grassland and as an arable weed, often growing in abundance in the first year, after the re-seeding of silage fields.

This species is best identified by the large, black blotch, which often occurs in the centre of the **lance-shaped** leaves. The tiny, pink flowers form several stout **flower-heads** on top of hairless, branched, sometimes reddish stems. Although superficially similar to Amphibious Bistort (opposite), the black leaf blotch and multiple **flower-heads** make Redshank easily distinguishable. Redshank is noticeable early on in the year, as its leaves are one of the first obvious signs of growth in the silage fields and recently re-seeded arable fields.

This species produces huge numbers of seeds. In the autumn and winter, these provide a vital food resource for birds such as Skylark, Twite and Rock Dove. An alternative Gaelic name, *Lus chrann cuesaidg* (Herb of the Tree of Crucifixion), stems from the belief that the blotches on the leaves were the blood falling from Christ's wounds.

Form: **sprawling** to **erect** 20cm-70cm.

Flowers: **flower-head**, 2cm-4cm long.

Leaves: **alternate, lance-shaped**, 5cm-10cm long.

Knotweed family

Bloody Crane's-bill *Geranium sanguineum/Creachlach Dearg*

Habitat: abundant on dunes in W Coll, but local elsewhere on the island. Rare on rock ledges on Tiree.

Although the individual flowers occur on long, solitary, downy stalks, this is a bushy, clump-forming species that, in the west of Coll at least, smothers the dune systems in a rich reddish-purple carpet. At the end of flowering, each of the five petals fall and the **sepals** become crimson red and are very obvious alongside the fruits. The distinctive bill-shaped fruit gives the plant its name.

The Gaelic name Creachlach Dearg means 'red wound healer' and relates directly to its medicinal properties.

Form: **erect** or **prostrate**, 20cm-30cm , (can reach 40cm).

Flowers: 2cm-3cm.

Leaves: **palmate**, with 5-7 deeply cut lobes.

Fruit: long 'bill'.

Crane's-bill family

Flowering: May - Sep

Ragged-Robin *Lychnis flos-cuculi*/Caorag Lèana

Habitat: widespread and common in all damp areas.

A distinctive and common flower found in damp places, appearing as a bright pink blaze in some fields. The flowers appear ragged, but each of the five petals is neatly split into four narrow lobes, whilst the fused **sepals** form a reddish **tube** behind the petals. Occasionally, plants can have white flowers. The slender stem bears slightly hairy **opposite** leaves, which often have a red tinge to the edge. Those at the top are narrower than those below, which are more **spoon shaped**. The distinctive fruit **capsules** split at the top into five teeth.

Form: **erect**, up to 50cm, (can reach 75cm).

Flowers: up to 4cm across.

Leaves: **opposite**, **sword** to **spoon shaped**, slightly hairy, up to 10cm long.

Fruit: up to 3cm long

As it was traditionally thought to bring bad luck if the flowers were cut and brought indoors, they were widely used instead for garlands and crowns. The flowers are attractive to a wide range of butterflies, hoverflies and long-tongued bees and are often pollinated by the Green-veined White Butterfly.

Pink family

Flowering: Jun - Oct   Seeds: Sep - Oct   65

Red Campion *Silene dioica*/Cìrean Coilich

Habitat: rare, only occurs naturally on sea cliff slopes at Ceann a' Mhara and Hynish, Tiree, although has been planted in gardens on Coll

Red Campion has attractive, deep pink flowers bearing five petals that are deeply notched and are borne on reddish stems. Very rarely, Red Campion can have white flowers, but it always lacks the obvious greenish 'bladders' beneath the flowers of Sea Campion (page 144). Both species have flask-shaped seed **capsules** in autumn. The large leaves are stalked at the base but stalkless on the stem.

Form:	**erect**, 50cm-100cm.
Flowers:	20mm-25mm across.
Leaves:	**opposite**, **tear drop shaped**, hairy, up to 25cm.

The plant has ancient connections to folklore and was associated with fairies. Picking flowers was considered to bring bad luck, which could involve snakes, goblins, devils and death – certainly the plant seems to favour treacherous locations on the Ceann a' Mhara cliffs.

Pink family

Flowering: May - Aug   Seeds: Sep

Marsh Cinquefoil *Potentilla palustris*/Coìg-bhileach Uisge

Habitat: common in marshes, bogs and on wet acidic ground.

The distinctive maroon-coloured flowers are dominated by five large, purplish, pointed **sepals** arranged in a star pattern, in between which lie the much smaller, more crimson-coloured petals. There is a small strawberry-like structure in the centre of the flower surrounded by a ring of crimson **stamens**, each tipped with a black **anther**. The distinctive leaves are **pinnate** with five to seven finger-like leaflets, bearing a finely **toothed** edge. Each appears on a short stalk with a papery **stipule** at its base. The leaves are grey-green in colour and are markedly paler on the undersurface.

Form: **creeping** to **erect**, up to 50cm.

Flowers: 2cm-3cm across.

Leaves: lower leaves **pinnate**, with 5-7 leaflets; upper leaves **palmate** to **trifoliate**; all leaves **toothed.**

Being a marshy plant, Marsh Cinquefoil has been used for millennia to cure fevers which prevailed in wet, ill-drained lands. Possibly because of its striking looks, it also features in traditions of magic: benignly, as a herb in love divination from the Middle Ages; usefully, as a special bait for fishing nets to ensure a heavy catch, and gruesomely, in a witch's ointment that included the fat of children dug up from the grave.

Rose family

Red Clover *Trifolium pratense*/Seamrag Dhearg

Habitat: common and widespread in grasslands including machair, pastures, meadows and on cliffs.

Red Clover is a prolific plant often lending a crimson hue to the grassy areas and the machair in particular. The **flower-heads** are initially tightly clustered, but can open out as the season progresses. Individual flowers are tubular with unequal, hairy **bracts**. Directly below the **flower-head** are three oval to bluntly **oval** leaflets, which are often marked with a white V-shape and have an obvious **midrib** on the underside. Although Red Clover usually appears upright, the plant stem can collapse under the weight of the **flower-head**.

Form: mostly **erect**, up to 30cm (can reach 60cm).

Flowers: flower-heads, 20mm-40mm; individual flower, 12mm-14mm

Leaves: alternate, oval to bluntly oval, 10mm-30mm.

leaflet

Red Clover is also known as 'Bee Bread' and is visited by long-tongued bumblebees. It is a beneficial plant, as it is nitrogen fixing and can be ploughed-in to fertilize the soil. It can be used as fodder for cattle (or humans - fresh, young leaves taste good in salads).

Pea family

68

Habitat: common and abundant around the coast.

Thrift, or Sea Pink, is a common and characteristic plant of the islands' coastlines. In spring, the rocks and salt marshes are ablaze with the nodding pink flowers, which consist of many tiny flowers in a tight ball-like head. The leaves are long, thin and slightly fleshy. Thrift can grow out of impossible looking crevices, and the woody rootstock can last for many years, forming a big, bouncy cushion. After flowering, the blooms can last for many weeks in a dried, brown state.

Form: **erect**, to 30cm.

Flowers: flower-head,
15mm-25mm across.

Leaves: **rosette**, **linear**,
2cm-15cm long.

Thrift was used on Tiree to treat barr a' chinn, a melancholy affliction of children. (see local stories, page 171-173). The common Gaelic name, Nèoinean Cladaich, translates as 'shore daisy', perhaps reflecting the abundance of Thrift on our coasts.

Thrift family

Lousewort *Pedicularis sylvatica*/Lus Riabhach Monaidh
Marsh Lousewort *Pedicularis palustris*/Lus Riabhach

Habitat: both louseworts are widespread on damp, acidic grasslands and heaths.

Lousewort

Form: **prostrate** to **erect**, up to 10cm (can reach 25cm).

Flowers: up to 25mm long

Leaves: **alternate**, oblong, deeply cut into **toothed** lobes, 1cm-2cm long.

Although superficially similar, the louseworts can be differentiated by both habitat and form. Marsh Lousewort appears in wetter areas and has longer leaves. Its single red stem resembles a small tree in the way it branches. Lousewort has many stems spreading from the base; it has a more inflated **calyx**, which is usually green, so it looks as though there are small "puffballs" below each flower. The flowers of both plants are tubular. Marsh Lousewort flowers are pink-purple with a four-toothed upper **lip**, while those of Lousewort are pink and have a two-toothed upper **lip**. The flowers may be confused with those of Red Bartsia (page 74).

Some maintain that louseworts are so named because of the belief that stock, grazed in lousewort-rich areas – with poor, damp, acidic soil - was more prone to parasites such as lice. Conversely, a 1760s "Report on the Hebrides" describes the pounded root of Marsh Lousewort being used to treat parasitic infestations. Untroubled by such worries, many children have called lousewort 'the Honey Flower', as nectar can be sucked from the blooms.

Marsh Lousewort

Form: **erect**, up to 20cm.

Flowers: up to 25mm long

Leaves: **alternate**, oblong, deely cut into **toothed** lobes, 1cm-5cm long.

Figwort family
Flowering: Lousewort, Apr - Jul   Marsh Lousewort, May - Aug

Cuckooflower *Cardamine pratensis*/Flùr na Cuthaig

Habitat: abundant and widespread in marshes and grasslands on both islands, often seen on roadsides.

Form: **erect**, up to 50cm (can reach 60cm).

Flowers: 6mm-18mm across.

Leaves: **basal rosette**, **pinnate** with round to **kidney shaped** leaflets; stem leaves, ladder-like; all slightly hairy.

Fruit: slender **pods** up to 4cm long.

The name Cuckooflower is derived from the timing of flowering, which coincides with the return of the Cuckoo in spring. It is also known as Lady's Smock, possibly in reference to the white form, which is said to resemble a milkmaid's smock. The plant is a close relative of the cabbage and is favoured by the caterpillars of several species of butterfly.

A familiar spring plant with attractive flowers that are clustered at the tip of the stem. There are four broad petals arranged in a cross which range in colour from deep pink to whitish lilac. The erect stem bears leaves with narrow, pointed leaflets arranged in ladders, whereas the lower leaves are reminiscent of Water-cress (page 148).

Cabbage family

Flowering: Apr - Jun

Marsh Willowherb *Epilobium palustre*/Seileachan Lèana
Hoary Willowherb *Epilobium parviflorum*/Seileachan Liath

Habitat: both species are frequent and widespread in wet places.

Marsh Willowherb

Form: limply **erect**, up to 30cm (can reach 60cm).

Flowers: up to 7mm across.

Leaves: **lance shaped**, to 8cm long and 1cm wide.

Both of the common small willowherbs on the islands have attractive pink flowers and the two plants can appear very similar at first glance. Marsh Willowherb is smaller, bearing just a few tiny, pale-pink flowers on weak, nodding stalks. The flowers of Hoary Willowherb appear a little earlier in the year; they are larger, open more fully and are often a richer pink. The leaves and stem are also useful identifying features, with Hoary Willowherb displaying abundant soft hairs on both. Hoary Willowherb, with its thicker stem and broader leaves, generally looks more robust than Marsh Willowherb. See also Great and Rosebay Willowherb, (page 54).

Hoary Willowherb

Form: **erect**, up to 60cm (can reach 75cm).

Flowers: up to 9mm across.

Leaves: **tear-drop shaped**, hairy, up to 12cm long and 4cm wide.

Willowherb family
Flowering: Marsh Willowherb: Jul - Sep   Hoary Willowherb: Jun - Aug

Red Dead-nettle *Lamium purpureum*/Caoch-dheanntag Dhearg

Habitat: frequent but local in waste ground, gardens and cultivated land.

The purplish-pink flowers of this familiar plant of cultivation grow in **whorls** at the top of reddish, bristly, branched stems. They have a hooded upper **lip** and a lower **lip** that is toothed at the base. All of the dark green, **heart-shaped** leaves are stalked and they often acquire a purplish tinge with age. Two similar species of dead-nettle occur on the islands. There are several subtle differences but simple things to note are that Cut-leaved Dead-nettle has much more deeply **toothed** upper leaves and Northern Dead-nettle has stalkless leaves. The louseworts (page 70), Marsh Woundwort (page 27), and Red Bartsia (page 74) are also superficially similar, but look closely and you will soon be able to identify them all!

Form: erect, or sprawling 10cm-30cm.

Flowers: 10mm-18mm long.

Leaves: **tear-drop** to **heart shaped,** short, rounded teeth.

Dead-nettle family

Red Bartsia *Odontites vernus*/Modhalan Coitcheann

Habitat: abundant on machair grasslands, meadows, along paths and as an arable weed.

A straggly, hairy and much-branched plant, with its pink flowers arranged on one side of slightly curved **spikes**. The flowers are neatly formed at the base of the upper leaves and are open-mouthed, with **stamens** that protrude like a tongue. They have a hooded upper **lip** and a lower **lip** that has three lobes. The unstalked leaves occur as **opposite** pairs, and the downy stems, which from a distance look dusty, are often tinged purplish. The **bracts** can also be purple and are smaller than the stem leaves. This species could be confused with the louseworts (page 70), but the shape of the leaves and the habitat are very different.

Form: erect to 10cm-30cm, can reach 50cm).

Flowers: 8mm-10mm long.

Leaves: opposite pairs, tear-drop shaped, toothed.

Red Bartsia is semi-parasitic on the roots of other plants, particularly grasses. It was once considered a cure for toothache. From this it gained its generic name *Odontites*, which comes from the Greek word for tooth, 'odons'. It was called bartsia by the 18th Century Swedish naturalist, Carl Linnaeus, after a close friend and fellow Swede, Dr. Bartoch.

Figwort family

Flowering: Jun - Sep   Leaves only: May

Dove's-foot Crane's-bill *Geranium molle* /Crobh Preachain Mìn
Common Stork's-bill *Erodium cicutarium*/Gob Corra

Habitat: Dove's-foot Crane's-bill is widespread on dunes and machair. Common Stork's-bill is frequent on dunes, machair and cultivated/disturbed ground.

Dove's-foot Crane's-bill

Form: **erect** or spreading, 20cm-30cm.

Flowers: 5mm-10mm across.

Leaves: **palmate**, with 5-7 deeply cut, slightly **toothed** lobes.

Fruit: long, 2cm-3cm, beak-like seed **pods**.

These two species are superficially similar in habitat, size, flower colour and hairiness. Common Stork's-bill usually has a loose head of larger flowers with rounded petals, and can sometimes show a blackish spot at the base of the upper two petals. Dove's-foot Crane's-bill flowers have deeply notched petals and appear in pairs. The structure of the seed heads is similar, but the flowers of Dove's-foot Crane's-bill appear at the end of short stalks, whilst Common Stork's-bill is long-stalked. Dove's-foot Crane's-bill has typical hairy, geranium-type leaves, recalling the shape of a dove's foot, while Common Stork's-bill has feathery, fern-like leaves and conspicuous narrow **stipules**. Both species have a beak-like seed **pod**, as seen in the photo below.

The seed of both species is dispersed over a distance of several feet by an explosive mechanism. Common Stork's-bill seeds are an important component of the diet of young Twite in late summer.

Common Stork's-bill

Form: **erect**, spreading or **prostrate**, 25cm-40cm, (can reach 60cm).

Flowers: 10mm-18mm across.

Leaves: **pinnate** with deeply cut fern-like leaflets.

Fruit: long, 2cm-4cm, beak-like seed **pods**.

Crane's-bill family

Common Centaury *Centaurium erythraea*/Ceud-bhileach

Habitat: common in sand dunes; fairly frequent and widespread in grassland on shallow sandy soils.

Common Centaury's pink flowers and yellow **stamens** stand out amongst the green grasses of its habitat. It has one or more stems, which can have many branches towards the top. The flowers appear in flat-topped clusters at the branch tips. The five petals are fused to form a relatively long **tube** at their base, spreading outwards at their tips to display the **stamens**. It is a common plant of the sand dunes, best seen in the early part of the day as the flowers often close up by late afternoon. The veined leaves are glossy and hairless.

Form: erect, up to 20cm, (can reach 50cm).

Flowers: 9mm-15mm across.

Leaves: **basal rosette, oval**; stem leaves shorter, pointed and paired.

Common Centaury is a bitter herb that increases stomach secretions, bile production and stimulates the appetite. As such it is known to strengthen the digestive function. It was used in the past to cure fevers and is currently in use both in Bach Flower Remedies and in homeopathic medicine. The Gaelic name translates as 'hundred leaves'. This arises from a misunderstanding of the Irish Gaelic, *ceadharlach*, meaning 'centaur', so named after the centaur Chiron who was reknowned for his skill with medicinal herbs.

Gentian family

Flowering: Jun - Sep

Pale Butterwort *Pinguicula lusitanica*/Mòthan Beag Bàn

Habitat: occasional in wet heath and bogs.

Pale Butterwort is a distinctive plant with a **rosette** of spreading leaves, which looks like a starfish. The leaves are oblong, are olive in colour with purple veins, and the leaf edges are rolled inwards. Stems bearing a solitary lilac-pink flower rise

up from the **rosette**. The flowers are made up of a five-lobed **tube**, which is open at mouth and has a yellow throat patch. The cylindrical **spur** is bent downwards and is blunt tipped. Pale Butterwort can be distinguished from its cousin, the Common Butterwort (page 41) by its smaller size, varying leaf colour and flower with a downwards pointing, rather than backwards pointing, **spur**.

Form: **erect**, 3cm-10cm, (can reach 15cm).

Flowers: 9mm-11mm long.

Leaves: **basal rosette**, oblong, 1cm-2cm long.

Butterworts are carnivorous plants with leaves that are covered in sticky glands that trap insects. The plant then digests the insect's soft tissue, thereby obtaining nutrients that are missing from the soil.

Bladderwort family

Flowering: Jun - Oct

Bog Pimpernel *Anagallis tenella*/Falcair Lèana

Habitat: locally common in damp grasslands and bogs.

Bog Pimpernel is a tiny creeping plant, often overlooked, as the stem winds between taller neighbours in damp grassland. When abundant, a mat of stems form, and the subtle beauty of the mass of delicate pinky flowers will reward those who look closely. The flowers, which only open when the sun is out, have short stalks and are funnel shaped. The five, lobed petals are actually white, but have crimson veins thereby appearing pink. The green leaves appear in pairs on short stalks along the stem.

Form: **creeping,** up to 2cm.

Flowers: up to 1cm long.

Leaves: **opposite, oval** to **circular,** up to 5mm long.

"No heart can think, no tongue can tell
The virtues of the pimpernel." (Grieve 1931).

The name *Anagallis* is derived from the Greek 'Anagelao', signifying 'to laugh', because the plant has been used to remove depression and dispel sadness.

Primrose family

Flowering: Jun - Aug

Scarlet Pimpernel *Anagallis arvensis* subsp. *arvensis/*
Falcair Sgàrlaid

Habitat: rare, in cultivated or disturbed ground.

Scarlet Pimpernel is a slender, annual plant of disturbed, sandy ground. The trailing, square stem has stalkless, oval leaves with black dots on their underside. The striking scarlet-red, wheel-shaped flowers have a dense fringe of tiny hairs on the five petals. The solitary flowers are held on slender stalks, which arise from the join of the leaf and the stem. The flowers open only on sunny days, and will close quickly if rain threatens.

Form:	**prostrate**, to 20cm, (can reach 40cm).
Flowers:	7mm-14mm across.
Leaves:	**opposite** pairs, **oval**, pointed, 5mm-20mm long.

Herbalists have used Scarlet Pimpernel for at least 2000 years - probably much longer - often in the treatment of melancholy, epilepsy, and related mental disorders. As with any strong medicine, old or new, there are dangers. In experiments it has exercised a strong narcotic effect on dogs, which killed some of them. The term 'the elusive Scarlet Pimpernel' (made famous by Baroness Orczy's book) reflects the fact that the flowers are often closed, and, as the plant is small, it is very difficult to find it when no scarlet is showing!

Primrose family

Flowering: Jun - Aug

Curled Dock *Rumex crispus*/Copag Chamagach
Common Sorrel *Rumex acetosa*/Samh
Sheep's Sorrel *Rumex acetosella*/Sealbhag nan Caorach

Habitat: All three species are common and widespread, occurring in cultivated fields, roadsides, grasslands and along the shore.

Curled Dock

Form:	**erect**, up to 100cm, (can reach 200cm).
Flowers:	2mm-6mm across.
Leaves:	**basal**, **alternate**, oblong to **lance shaped**, up to 40cm long.
Fruit:	dry and flat; redden with age.

These three plants are superficially similar, but can be distinguished primarily by their overall size and by differences in the shape of their leaves. Sheep's Sorrel is the smallest of the three. Its stalked leaves are small, oblong and have two forwardly-pointing lobes at the base forming a **arrow shaped**. The long-stalked leaves of Common Sorrel are larger, becoming redder with age, and the basal lobes point downwards, making the leaf more **spear shaped**. The stem leaves of Curled Dock are longer still, with distinctly crimped, wavy edges and a bold **mid-rib**. The fruits of the Curled Dock are greener and rounded, whilst those of the two Sorrels are redder and triangular in shape. The flowers of all three plants are tiny and green and are arranged in tight **whorls**.

Common Sorrel

The male and female flowers of Sheep's Sorrel are borne on different plants, although they look identical. Common Sorrel has a sharp acid taste, which was once favoured in salads, unlike Sheep's Sorrel, which was regarded as a salad plant fit only for sheep!

Common Sorrel

Form:	**erect**, up to 60cm, (can reach 100cm).
Flowers:	2mm-6mm across.
Leaves:	**basal**, **alternate**, and **spear shaped**, up to 20cm long.
Fruit:	dry and flat; redden with age.

Sheep's Sorrel

Form:	**erect**, up to 20cm, (can reach 30cm).
Flowers:	2mm-6mm across.
Leaves:	**basal**, **alternate**, and **arrow shaped**, up to 10cm long.
Fruit:	dry and flat; redden with age.

Knotweed family
Curled Dock: Jun - Oct

Flowering:
Common Sorrel: May - Jun   Sheep's Sorrel: May -

Sea-milkwort *Glaux maritima*/Lus na Saillteachd

Habitat: common and widespread on rocky shores and salt marshes.

The diminutive Sea-milkwort is locally very common at the top of beaches, where it often creeps amongst other vegetation. It can also occur in dense strands of its own. The arrangement of the small, stalkless leaves in rows is unusual. The stalkless pink flowers are cooried (nestled) in to the join between the leaves and the stem. The flower consists of five **sepals** and five **stamens**, but no petals. The fleshy leaves and succulent stem help conserve moisture.

Form: **prostrate**, to 15cm, (can reach 30cm).

Flowers: 4mm-6mm across.

Leaves: overlapping and arranged in 4 rows, pointedly oblong, 4mm-12mm long.

The fleshy leaves have been used in pickles. The Gaelic translates as 'plant of saltiness'.

Primrose family

Montbretia *Crocosmia*/Fochann Innseanach

Habitat: a garden escapee, which is now widespread and rather frequent amongst rocks and on road sides.

The very attractive vivid orange flowers are funnel shaped, with a wide spreading **corolla**, and are quite unlike any other flower on the islands. The distinctive clumps of long, sword-like, dark green leaves persist through the winter, and develop from small, persistent corms (a modified underground stem, like a bulb).

Form: **erect**, up to 60cm, (can reach 120cm).

Flowers: up to 31cm long.

Leaves: **sword like**, up to 60cm long.

This is an increasingly common introduced plant in Britain and one that may eventually be targeted for localised removal in order to prevent it swamping large areas of native vegetation. Although not a wild flower, it has been included in this book as it is so commonly seen on roadsides, particularly on Tiree.

Iris family

82   Flowering: Jul - Sep   Leaves only: Dec - Jun

Introduction to the yellow-brown section

Everyone knows a buttercup. Along with the Daisy, it is one of the first flowers you recognise in childhood, but did you know that there are three different species? Everyone can recognise a Dandelion, but what you are seeing as a Dandelion may well be Autumn Hawkbit, Smooth Hawk's-beard or Cat's-ear! The buttercup family are an easy species to begin the journey into a greater understanding of botany. As you start to become aware of the different leaf shapes and position of sepals, for example, you will surprise yourself with your ability to differentiate between what once seemed a homogenous group. I have spent years thinking that Lesser Spearwort, which grows in abundance right outside my gate, was a buttercup. In learning to look at the leaves it was with a sense of pride that I now name them correctly.

When explaining my thinking behind this book, I have described it as functioning on three levels. The first is to introduce many of the 'top-level' species that you are immediately aware of as you wander the islands during spring and summer: Yellow Iris, Gorse or Primrose. The second level is to increase awareness of the island specialities, such as Elecampane on Tiree or Spotted Rock-rose on Coll, plus the less easily seen species--the ones that you don't notice until you have grasped the top level, such as Lesser Meadow-rue or Pineappleweed. The third level is to really get your teeth into specific identifications, to be able to tell the Common from the Greater Bird's-foot-trefoil and to separate these two from Meadow Vetchling.

Why is this important? Personally it brings me great pleasure, but it also brings a deeper appreciation of the natural world. With this comes an increased respect, which can't be a bad thing, (although no one can persuade me that Mugwort is anything but ugly).

Common Ragwort

Mugwort *Artemisia vulgaris*/Liath-lus

Habitat: an occasional, but locally common weed of dunes and disturbed ground such as arable fields, waste places and roadsides.

A tall, late-flowering, aromatic plant of waste places. The clustered flowers are small and inconsequential, with dominant pale grey **bracts**. The numerous, tiny **flower-heads** open yellow, but quickly turn reddish-brown. The tough, woody stem bears distinct grooves and is tinged reddish. The distinctive, delicate **basal** leaves are finely lobed and stalked. The upper leaves are stalkless. All the leaves are dark green above, but silvery white below and bear pronounced veins and a green edge.

Form: **erect**, up to 150cm.

Flowers: 3mm–4mm across.

Leaves: **basal**, deeply cut into many lobes; stem leaves, oblong to **lance-shaped** lobes; all leaves up to 8cm long.

Mugwort is so-called as it was formerly used to keep away midges; the slight, but distinctive, scent is apparently a deterrent to these formidable biting insects. In Orkney, Mugwort stems are used to weave baskets for use at sea.

Daisy family

Flowering: Jul - Sep   Leaves only: Jun

Yellow Iris *Iris pseudacorus*/Seileasdair

Habitat: widespread and abundant in damp grassland and along the edges of ditches and streams.

This is a very common plant of damp pastures. Its distinctively tall, flat, grey-green leaves have a raised central **mid-rib** and grow up inside each other from underground **rhizomes**; they are one of the first signs of spring on the islands. The large flowers, which are supported by a large, green **bract**, consist of three bright yellow, drooping petals, plus three smaller, erect, yellow petals. When mature, the large, drooping, oblong green fruit splits into three parts, each carrying a row of hard, orange-brown seeds.

seed capsule

Form: **erect**, 30cm-70cm, (can reach 150cm).

Flowers: up to 10cm across.

Leaves: **sword shaped**, up to 1m long.

Fruit: large, oblong **capsule**.

This plant provides important early cover for Corncrakes to hide in when they return to the islands in late April. Most other vegetation is still too short. The word 'iris' is the name of the goddess of the rainbow in Greek mythology and refers to the wide range of colours exhibited by different species of iris.

Iris family

Flowering: May - Aug   Leaves only: Feb - Apr, Oct   Seeds: Aug - Sep   85

Honeysuckle *Lonicera periclymenum*/Lus na Meala

Habitat: rare on rock ledges and amongst gorse on Tiree, more frequent in rocky gullies and roadside verges on Coll.

Honeysuckle is a highly attractive flower with a delightful scent. The plant has long trailing stems, which grow over rock ledges or high into Gorse (page 108), in places where livestock cannot graze. The flowers have two **lips** and are trumpet shaped. They occur in clusters of up to twelve and darken as they mature from white, to cream, to peach. The wild plants on the islands are very similar to varieties that are widely cultivated in gardens.

Form: **trailing**, up to 6m (can reach 10m).

Flowers: up to 5cm long.

Leaves: **opposite**, **oval**, 3cm-7cm long.

Fruit: bright red berries.

The fragrant scent of the flowers attracts hawk-moths at night, whose tongues are long enough to probe the slender flowers. The berries are poisonous to humans, but are attractive to birds.

Honeysuckle family

Flowering: May - Jul   Berries: Aug - Sep

Elecampane *Inula helenium*/Ailleann

Habitat: occasional and local on roadside verges and around crofts in West Tiree.

Elecampane is a large and striking plant which is unlikely to be confused with any other flowers on the islands. It has large, golden yellow, daisy-like flowers and broadly **lance-shaped** to **heart-shaped** leaves. The plant was introduced to Tiree over 100 years ago for medicinal purposes (see below) and was widely planted around crofts. It currently occurs in at least ten widely scattered localities around the western half of the island, but is absent from Coll.

Form: **erect**, 50cm-150cm (can reach 250cm).

Flowers: 6mm-9mm across.

Leaves: broadly **lance shaped** to **heart shaped**, up to 40cm long and 30cm wide, with wavy edges.

According to fable, Elecampane came from the tears shed by Helen of Troy when Paris stole her away at the start of the Trojan wars, hence the Latin name. The plant is frequently mentioned as a valuable herb by ancient writers such as Pliny, and by Anglo-Saxon herbalists prior to the Norman Conquest. Amongst its many medicinal uses, it was mainly used for chest complaints such as whooping cough and bronchitis in humans, and for skin complaints in sheep and horses, hence the colloquial names of 'Scabwort' and 'Horse-heal'.

Daisy family

Perennial Sow-thistle *Sonchus arvensis*/Blioch Fochainn
Prickly Sow-thistle *Sonchus asper*/Searbhan Muice
Smooth Sow-thistle *Sonchus oleraceus*/Bainne Muice

Habitat: all three species are widespread in waste places, in cultivated land and along the coast. Prickly Sow-thistle is the most frequent, whilst Smooth Sow-thistle is scarcer, but may have been overlooked.

Perennial Sow-thistle

Form: erect, up to 120cm, (can reach 150cm).

Flowers: up to 5cm across.

Leaves: **alternate**, deeply cut into **toothed** lobes, long, tapering end lobe; entire leaf up to 40cm long.

Prickly Sow-thistle

Form: erect, up to 100cm, (can reach 150cm).

Flowers: up to 3cm across.

Leaves: **alternate**, deeply cut into prickly lobes; entire leaf up to 30cm long.

Daisy family

These three plants are very similar, all having flat-topped, yellow, Dandelion-like **composite flower-heads** and leaves that clasp the stem. Prickly Sow-thistle can be distinguished by its hairless stem and tough glossy-green leaves, which are edged with hard prickly spines. Perennial Sow-thistle also has leaf spines, but these are softer and merely bristly, whilst the larger flowers are more golden yellow in the centre, and there are sticky yellow hairs on the **sepal**-like **bracts**. Smooth Sow-thistle, as its names suggests, lacks any spines on the leaves, which, in addition, have pointed **auricles** at their base, as opposed to the rounded **auricles** of the other two. All species have a milky sap in their stems and leaves.

The *Really Wild Food Guide* recommends a recipe for 'Braised Sow-thistle and Button Mushrooms' (Jumbalaya 2002). In the USA all the sow–thistles are invasive species and are widespread.

Smooth Sow-thistle

Form: **erect**, up to 100cm, (can reach 150cm).

Flowers: up to 3cm across.

Leaves: **alternate**, deeply cut into toothed lobes; entire leaf up to 40cm long.

Colt's-foot *Tussilago farfara*/Cluas Liath

Habitat: locally common in sand dunes and some roadsides.

Colt's-foot has stout, scaly, purplish stolons (stems that are either erect or lie loosely on the ground) and grows in sand dunes often very close to the sea. It is a distinctive **perennial** herb, with yellow flowers that can be seen in very early spring. The hoof-shaped leaves appear later. They have long stalks and are downy above and white felted below.

Form: **prostrate** to **erect**, up to 15cm.

Flowers: **flower-head**, 15mm–35mm across.

Leaves: 20cm across, hoof shaped.

Colt's-foot leaves have been smoked for thousands of years and are still the main ingredient in herbal 'tobacco'. Whether smoked, drunk as tea, or used as syrup, it is renowned for helping coughs, asthma and other lung problems. The white-felted hairs on the leaves can be dried and used as tinder, while the fluffy seedheads have been used to stuff pillows.

Daisy family

Flowering: Feb - Apr   Leaves only: Apr - Jul

Common Ragwort *Senecio jacobaea*/Buaghallan
Marsh Ragwort *Senecio aquaticus*/Caoibhreachan

Habitat: Common Ragwort is frequent and widespread on dunes, machair and field margins, more so on Tiree.
Marsh Ragwort is frequent and widespread in wet habitats.

Common Ragwort

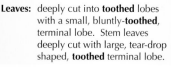

Form: **erect**, up to 100cm.

Flowers: 15mm-25mm across.

Leaves: deeply cut into **toothed** lobes with a small, bluntly-**toothed**, terminal lobe. Stem leaves deeply cut with large, tear-drop shaped, **toothed** terminal lobe.

These two common species are very similar, although they generally prefer somewhat different habitats. The flowers of Common Ragwort normally consist of thirteen golden **rays** and are carried in dense, flat-topped clusters. Marsh Ragwort flowers are larger, with thirteen to twenty golden **rays**, but there are fewer of them and they are more open. The inner **bracts** also differ, those on Marsh Ragwort being sharply pointed and having white edges, those of Common Ragwort being dark-tipped. The leaves, too, are different. Although both have deeply-cut stem leaves, Marsh Ragwort's are glossy, and the terminal lobe is much larger. Common Ragwort only occasionally has purple stems, but for Marsh Ragwort this is often the case.

Ragwort is an important nectar source for insects, particularly hoverflies and Burnet Moths. Both species are poisonous to livestock, if eaten in large quantities. On Tiree, there are plans to control the spread of the highly invasive Common Ragwort. Both ragworts are biennial.

Marsh Ragwort

base leaf

Form: **erect**, up to 80cm.

Flowers: 20mm-35mm across.

stem leaf

Leaves: lower leaves with large, egg-shaped, slightly **toothed** terminal lobe. Stem leaves deeply cut with large, tear-drop shaped, **toothed** terminal lobe.

Daisy family

Common

Marsh

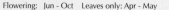

Flowering: Jun - Oct   Leaves only: Apr - May

Corn Marigold *Chrysanthemum segetum*/Bile Bhuide

Habitat: locally abundant on cultivated machair on Tiree only.

Corn Marigold is a member of the daisy family, and has inner and outer **florets** that are completely golden-yellow. It has a branched stem and its leaves are grey-green and slightly fleshy. The lower leaves have a winged stalk, while the upper leaves clasp the stem. Corn Marigold is an annual plant, favouring recently cultivated fields. It can put on an extraordinary display of colour and vitality, akin to an arable field glowing with poppies.

Form: **erect**, to 50cm.

Flowers: 35mm-65mm across.

Leaves: **alternate**, oblong, deeply **toothed.**

Corn Marigold was once seen as such a problem weed on arable ground that tenants were fined if they didn't eradicate it. With modern farming technology, Corn Marigolds - like many other annual flowers of arable fields - have become very scarce.

Daisy family

Flowering: Jun - Sep

Kidney Vetch *Anthyllis vulneraria*/Cas an Uain

Habitat: common and widespread on dunes, machair and on rocky coastal outcrops.

A common machair flower that often forms dense patches on slopes. It is mostly yellow but individual flowers can vary in colour from cream to red · even within a single **flower-head**. Although similar to Common and Greater Bird's-foot-trefoil (page 109), Kidney Vetch can be identified by its white woolly **sepals** at the base of the rather robust **flower-head** and by the ladder-like **pinnate** leaves, which bear a longer leaflet at the tip. In addition, the seed **pods** are minute.

Form: loosely **erect**, up to 25cm (can reach 60cm).

Flowers: flower-head is 2cm-4cm across.

Leaves: alternate, pinnate with ladder-like leaflets; entire leaf up to 10cm long.

This plant was widely known through Europe as a remedy for wounds and skin eruptions, possibly thanks to the absorbent nature of its woolly **flower-heads**. The kidney-shaped **flower-heads**, which give the plant its name, are also very attractive to bumble-bees, including the rare Great Yellow Bumble-bee. The Gaelic translates as 'lamb's foot', perhaps in reference to the small seed pod.

Pea family

Dandelion *Taraxacum officinale agg.*/Beàrnan Brìde
Smooth Hawk's-beard *Crepis capillaris*/Lus Curain Mìn

Habitat: Dandelion is widespread and common in grassy places, particularly in dunes, on lawns and along roadsides. Smooth Hawk's-beard is common in grassy places throughout the islands, particularly along roadsides, where it forms small colonies.

Dandelion

Form: **erect**, up to 20cm (can reach 30cm).

Flowers: **flower-head** up to 45mm across.

Leaves: **basal rosette,** deeply **toothed** and lobed, up to 25cm long.

Fruit: familiar fluffy clock of seeds.

leaf

The Dandelion is a very familiar plant, which flowers throughout the summer and can form a yellow swathe on lawns in spring. The yellow, flat-topped flowers are more orange centrally and bear a ruff formed by the re-curved lower **bracts**. The green **bracts** of Smooth Hawk's-beard alternate between short and long, the outermost of which are re-curved. Dandelion stems are reddish and unbranched, and the soft **basal** leaves bear a distinctive, pale central rib. Smooth Hawk's-beard has taller stems that are multi-branched and has both **basal** and stem leaves. Those higher up the stem are **arrow shaped**, taper to a fine point, have toothed edges and clasp the stem with their pointed **basal** lobes. There is also a **basal rosette** of lobed, **toothed** hairless leaves. Smooth Hawk's-beard has similar, but smaller, flowers, with **florets** that are tinged red on the underside tips. The seeds of both species have familiar parachute-like plumes to carry them on the wind.

Smooth Hawk's-beard

Form: **erect**, up to 60cm (can reach 80cm).

Flowers: **flower-head** 10mm-15mm wide.

Leaves: **basal** and stem, **alternate**, **pinnate**, up to 15cm long.

stem leaf   basal leaf

Daisy family

Dandelion: Flowering: Mar - Nov   Seeds: Jun - Nov
Smooth Hawk's-beard: Flowering: Jun - Sep   Seeds: Aug - Sep

Cat's-ear *Hypochaeris radicata*/Cluas Cait
Autumn Hawkbit *Leontodon autumnalis*/Caisearbhan Garbh

Habitat: Cat's-ear is frequent and widespread in grasslands, often favouring dunes, rocks and waste places.
Autumn Hawkbit is abundant and widespread in grassland, including salt marshes.

Cat's-ear

Form: **erect**, up to 30cm (can reach 60cm).

Flowers: 2cm–4cm across.

Leaves: **basal rosette**, oblong, broadly **toothed**, to 15cm long. leaf

The flowers of both plants are yellow, flat topped and **rayed**. They are very similar to each other and to the Dandelion (opposite). Autumn Hawkbit is generally a smaller, neater plant, with red-striped rays on the underside of the flower, as opposed to the greenish-tinge of Cat's-ear. The leaves are also distinctive. Both plants are slightly branched (unlike the Dandelion) and bear similar fluffily hairy, dandelion-like fruit.

Cat's-ear is named after the tiny, scale-like, dark-tipped bracts on the stem, which resemble miniature cats' ears. You may see other Dandelion-like flowers growing on rock outcrops and dunes in West Coll, including a complex group called hawkweeds. The leaf of Mouse-ear Hawkweed is shown here.

Mouse-ear Hawkweed leaf

Autumn Hawkbit

Form: **erect**, up to 20cm (can reach 60cm).

Flowers: 2cm–4cm across.

Leaves: **basal rosette**, deeply cut into narrow lobes, hairless, up to 15cm long.

leaf

Daisy family

Flowering: Cat's-ear: May - Aug

Flowering: Autumn Hawkbit: Jun - Oct

95

Primrose *Primula vulgaris*/Sòbhrach

Habitat: occasionally abundant in grassland, particularly in dunes and on cliffs.

This classic flower of woods and gardens can be a real surprise when found carpeting the sand dunes or sea cliffs in early spring. Individual flowers have five notched, pale yellow petals, and appear on woolly stalks in a cluster from the distinctive **rosette** of wrinkled leaves. The stalkless leaves are hairless above and hairy below. Each plant has flowers that can either be "pin-eyed" (pin-head like **styles** visible at the **corolla**-mouth, with **stamens** hidden in the **tube** below) or "thrum-eyed" (long **stamens** visible at the **corolla**-mouth, with a short **style** hidden in the **tube** below).

Form: **erect**, up to 10cm.

Flowers: 3cm across.

Leaves: **basal rosette**, **spoon shaped**, 5cm-10cm long.

Charles Darwin first deduced that this flower arrangement (pin-eye and thrum-eye) allowed cross-pollination by bees. Primrose tea, drunk in the month of May, is famous for curing the 'phrensie' (hypochondria), and Primrose has been used to treat infections such as coughs or abscesses.

Primrose family

Flowering: Mar - Jun

Roseroot *Sedum rosea*/Lus nan Laoch

Habitat: locally frequent on sea cliffs on Coll, but rare on Tiree.

This cliff-loving member of the stonecrop family, with succulent leaves and yellow-brown flowers, is very distinctive. Each individual flower has four petals and forms slightly domed **flower-heads**. The greyish leaves overlap one another up the orangey stem and are often tinged purplish at the tips. There are separate male and female plants. The male flower has **stamens** and petals longer than its **sepals**. The female flower has petals and **sepals** of equal length and develops into an orange fruit, which is superficially like the flowers.

> **Form:** **erect**, 20cm-30cm.
>
> **Flowers:** 5mm-8mm across.
>
> **Leaves: alternate**, **oval**, slightly **toothed.**
>
> **Fruit:** follicles

Roseroot was used on calves in the Outer Hebrides for treating stomach disorders and on Skye as a spring purge. The Inuit ferment the plant for use as a famine food.

Stonecrop family

Flowering: May - Aug   Leaves only: Apr, Jul - Sep   Seeds: Aug - Sep

Lady's Bedstraw *Galium verum*/Lus an Leasaich

Habitat: widespread and abundant on machair and sand dunes.

Lady's Bedstraw has small, bright yellow flowers, clustered together in dense, branching **racemes** at the tops of the wiry stems, which sometimes appear square. Eight to ten tiny, dark green, narrow leaves gather together in numerous **whorls** at intervals up the hairy stem. In July and August the machair is filled with this gorgeous plant.

Form: **creeping** to **erect**, 15cm to 60cm.

Flowers: 2mm-3mm across.

Leaves: **whorl**, **linear**, 6mm-25mm long.

Lady's Bedstraw, or Our Lady's Bedstraw, is named from the story that this was a 'Cradle Herb', in the hay in the manger in Bethlehem. Like other bedstraws, it can also be used to curdle milk and make cheese. The Gaelic name reflects this use, translating as 'the rennet herb'. The small roots are a source for an orange-red dye, much harvested in the Hebrides for the tweed industry in the 18th Century.

Bedstraw family

Flowering: Jun - Sep

Spotted Rock-rose *Tuberaria guttata* subsp. *breweri*

Habitat: rare at just one location on Coll on shallow soil over a
gneiss outcrop.

This flower superficially resembles a hairy buttercup (page 104/5). However, its five yellow petals have a characteristic blood-red spot at their base, and the **sepals** are unequal and black dotted. The petals only open on sunny days and are often dropped by mid-day, in which case the distinguishing **sepals** may provide the best clue. The downy leaves have three veins and grow as a **basal rosette** and as **opposite** pairs up the stem.

When discovered on Coll in 2004, this was the first record for Scotland. 32 plants were recorded in 2004, and this had increased to 35 by 2006 Spotted Rock-rose occurs in the Channel Islands and western mainland

Europe; however, the subspecies *breweri* has a very limited distribution (three locations in western Ireland, two in North Wales and one site on Coll). As this is a new discovery for Scotland, there is not a Scottish Gaelic name yet. The Irish Gaelic is Grianros breac.

Form:	**erect,** 6cm-20cm, (can reach 30cm).
Flowers:	10mm-15mm across.
Leaves:	**basal rosette** and **opposite** pairs on stem, **oval** to **lance-shaped**, 4cm-6cm long.

Rock-rose family

Flowering: June

Habitat: widespread and common on machair.

Yellow-rattle has a square, dark-spotted stem, with **opposite** pairs of unstalked leaves. The flowers appear in short, leafy spikes and consist of yellow upper and lower **lips** and a flattened **calyx**, which inflates and becomes bladder-like when in fruit. The upper **lip** is flattened on a vertical plane and has two tiny, violet teeth. The lower **lip** is three lobed. The similar species, Common Cow-wheat, is relatively frequent on the uplands of Coll, but can be easily differentiated from Yellow-rattle as the leaves are untoothed and their habitats are very different.

Form: **erect**, up to 50cm.

Flowers: 15mm long.

Leaves: **opposite**, triangular in outline, coarsely **toothed**, 2cm-3cm long.

Fruit: bladder like.

Yellow-rattle is so named because the large seeds 'rattle' in the dry **calyx** when ripe. Like other members of its family, e.g. Eyebright (page 154), Yellow-rattle is a semi-parasite that extracts nourishment from grass roots.

Figwort family

Flowering: May - Sep   Seeds: Jun - Oct

Pineappleweed *Matricaria discoidea*/Lus Anainn
Tansy *Tanacetum vulgare*/Lus na Frainge

Habitat: Pineappleweed is a common and widespread weed of tracks and disturbed ground. Tansy is a local weed of roadside verges, and is a garden escapee.

Pineappleweed

Form: **erect** (often bushy), 20cm-40cm.

Flowers: flower-head, 5mm-10mm across.

Leaves: finely divided, feathery.

Pineappleweed is a familiar weed with clusters of cone-shaped **flower-heads** of dull, yellowish-green **florets**. Tansy is a much taller, more robust plant with clusters of golden-yellow, button-like **flower-heads**. The leaves of Pineappleweed are bright green, feathery and smell of pineapple. In fact, you can easily distinguish these plants if you lightly crush their leaves and inhale! Typical of other plants in the daisy family (e.g. Oxeye Daisy, page 138 or Coltsfoot, page 90), Pineappleweed and Tansy have heads of tiny **florets** rather than 'classic' flowers, but, in the case of these two species, only the **disc floret** is present, not the **ray floret**, which gives them the unusual appearance of having no petals.

Tansy

Form: **erect**, 40cm-120cm.

Flowers: flower-head, 7mm-12mm across.

Leaves: **alternate**, finely **pinnate** with **toothed** leaflets, large.

Daisy family

Lesser Celandine *Ranunculus ficaria*/Searragaich
Marsh-marigold *Caltha palustris*/Lus Buidhe Bealltainn

Habitat: Lesser Celandine is widespread and common on rock ledges cliffs and in grassland. Marsh-marigold is common in ditches, marshe and at the edge of lochs.

Lesser Celandine

Form: **creeping** to **erect**, up to 20cm

Flowers: 1cm-3cm across.

Leaves: **heart shaped** on long stalks, 4cm across.

The yellow flowers of these two common plants are amongst the earliest to appear and are welcome signs of spring. Both have buttercup-like flowers, but the two plants are easily separated. Marsh-marigold is a larger plant, with large, golden-yellow flower containing five petal-like **sepals**, whilst Lesser Celandine is smalle and its small flowers contain between eight and twelve pointe petals, which only open fully in bright sunshine, and are frequentl bleached whiter. The glossy leaves of the two plants are structurall similar, but those of Marsh-marigold are much larger, have a more strongly **toothed** edge and are almost stalkless higher up the stem.

Although most of the buttercup family are poisonous when fresh archaeologists in the Hebrides have uncovered many charred tubers o Lesser Celandine in Mesolithic deposits. Indigenous North American exploit them for food, after cooking, so perhaps the ancient Scots did so too. Or possibly they used them for another purpose - Lesser Celandine is also known as pilewort, very effective for haemorrhoids!

Marsh-marigold

Form: **creeping** to **erect**, up to 45cm

Flowers: 1cm-5cm across.

Leaves: **kidney shaped**, 10cm across, **toothed**.

 Lesser Celandine

Marsh-marigold

Buttercup family

Flowering: Feb - May

Lesser Spearwort *Ranunculus flammula*/Glaisleun

Habitat: very common and widespread in all wetter habitats.

Lesser Spearwort is often overlooked, as its flowers are the typical yellow buttercup flower. It is a member of the buttercup family and is very widespread in wet areas. Its **lance-shaped** leaves, with stalkless stem leaves and stalked **basal** leaves, and its smaller flowers, distinguish it from other buttercups (pages 104-105). Additionally, the flower stalks are furrowed, unlike those of the much rarer Greater Spearwort, which has unfurrowed flower stalks.

Form: **creeping** or **erect**, to 50cm.

Flowers: 7mm-20mm across.

Leaves: oblong to **lance shaped.**

When the roots or leaves are ground with salt, the resultant mixture causes skin to blister. 'Blistering', where blisters were raised to draw out 'humours', was once a common treatment. On the islands, this was achieved by grinding Lesser Spearwort leaves in a mortar, then applying the plant in a limpet shell to where the blister was to be raised. An account in 1767 reports "it is inconvenient...because it is very difficult to stop the discharge of serum which it occasions." (Milliken & Bridgewater 2004).

Meadow Buttercup *Ranunculus acris*/Buidheag an t-Samhraid

Bulbous Buttercup *Ranunculus bulbosus*/Fuile-thalmhainn

Creeping Buttercup *Ranunculus repens*/Buidheag

Habitat: common and widespread.

Meadow Buttercup

Form:	**erect**, up to 100cm.

Flowers: 2cm-3cm across.

Leaves: deeply 3-5 lobed, and lobes deeply **toothed.**

Buttercups are intensely acrid, hence the name *Ranunculus acris*. The juice of the plants can cause pain and blisters, and this fiery and hot-spirited nature was used to cure warts and to help with gout and shingles. Bulbous Buttercup is named after the bulb-like corm at its base.

Bulbous Buttercup

Form: **erect**, up to 40cm.

Flowers: 2cm-3cm across.

Leaves: 3 lobed, and lobes in **toothed** segments.

Buttercup family

Buttercups are some of our commonest and best known flowers, but distinguishing the many species requires care. All the yellow flowers are very similar, but the **sepals** under a Bulbous Buttercup are reflexed (point down). The Creeping and Meadow Buttercup can be separated by looking at the flower-stalk, which is grooved in the Creeping and not grooved in the Meadow. Other features include the leaves, which have increasing levels of deep cuts and divisions, from Creeping to Bulbous to Meadow. Only the Creeping Buttercup has runners.

sepals of Meadow Buttercup

Creeping Buttercup leaf

Creeping Buttercup

Form: **erect**, up to 60cm.

Flowers: 2cm-3cm across.

Leaves: 3 lobed, and lobes cut into 3 **toothed** segments.

Flowering: Meadow & Creeping: May - Aug   Bulbous: Apr - Jun

Silverweed *Potentilla anserina*/Brisgean

Habitat: widespread on sand dunes, shingle, roadside verges and bare ground.

Although from a distance Silverweed can be easily confused with buttercups (page 104/105), it becomes immediately recognisable when a green leaf is turned over and the downy, silver underside is exposed. The reddish, rooting stems creeping over the ground can also be obvious. Like a buttercup, Silverweed has long-stalked, yellow flowers with five petals, which are solitary, but the leaves are entirely different, comprising coarsely **toothed** leaflets.

Form: **creeping**, to 50cm long.

Flowers: 15mm-20mm across.

Leaves: **pinnate** with **alternate**, oblong, feathery leaflets.

In 1777, J. Lightfoot recorded Silverweed roots being used as a food source in his book *Flora Scotia*: "In the islands of Tirey and Col they are much esteemed, as answering in some measure the purposes of bread, they having been known to support inhabitants for months together during a scarcity of other provisions. They put a yolk on their ploughs, and often tear up their pasture grounds, with a view to eradicate the roots for their use; and in seasons that succeed the worst for other crops, so they never fail to afford a most seasonable relief to the inhabitants in times of the greatest scarcity. A singular instance of the bounty of providence to these islands."

Rose family

Flowering: Jun - Aug

Slender St. John's-wort *Hypericum pulchrum/*
Lus Chaluim Chille
Square-stalked St. John's-wort *Hypericum tetrapterum/*
Beachnuadh Fireann

Habitat: Slender St. John's-wort is occasional in non-**calcareous** grasslands, while Square-stalked St. John's-wort is occasional in damp places by water.

Slender St. John's-wort

Form: **erect,** up to 20cm, (can reach 60cm).

Flowers: 15mm across.

Leaves: opposite, bluntly **oval** to **heart shaped**.

The St John's-wort family includes about a dozen UK species, and as a family is easily recognisable. The yellow flowers are distinctive with five **sepals**, five petals, and a mass of large, reddish **stamens**. The leaves are always **opposite**, **untoothed** and stalkless, with translucent veins. The two species on this page can be distinguished by close examination of the stems and flowers. Slender St. John's-wort has a round, slender, reddish stem and distinguishing black dots on its **sepals**, while Square-stalked has a four-winged square stem, more pointed **sepals** and its flowers are pale yellow, rather than orange-yellow. See also Marsh St. John's-wort (page 111).

The Gaelic name, 'Lus Chaluim Chille', refers to St Columba from Iona. The story goes that St Columba gave St. John's-wort to a scared shepherd boy and told him to place it under his arm. The boy was never afraid again.

Square-stalked St. John's-wort

Form: **erect,** up to 40cm, (can reach 60cm).

Flowers: 10mm across.

Leaves: opposite, oval.

St. John's-wort family

Slender

Flowering: Jun - Aug

Square-stalked

107

Gorse *Ulex europaeus*/Conasg

Habitat: occasional and local on Tiree, but more common on Coll.

Gorse has deep yellow, pea-like flowers, which have a beautiful smell of coconut. The leaves are rigid, deeply grooved spines, which have smaller spines at intervals along their length (although the leaves of a newly emerging Gorse plant are soft). Gorse stems are woody and intricately twisted. The plant is well suited to acidic sandy heath and can flower all year round. Hence "When gorse is in flower, kissing is in season." However, the flowers are most striking from January to May.

Form:	spreading to **erect** shrub, up to 200cm, (can reach 250cm).
Flowers:	12mm-18mm.
Leaves:	spines.
Fruit:	black **pod** with brown or grey hairs.

Gorse provides nesting sites for small birds, which is particularly important on these relatively tree-less islands. This plant has a multitude of practical uses, many of which are listed in the First Statistical Account (from surveys conducted during the late 18th and early 19th centuries). It has been used as stock-proof fencing and can be fodder for horses, sheep and cattle, for which it is said to increase milk yield and expel worms. The dry spines make excellent kindling and, when tied in bundles, it was used to clear chimneys.

Pea family

  Flowering: all year

Common Bird's-foot-trefoil *Lotus corniculatus/*
Barra-mhìslean Lèana
Greater Bird's-foot-trefoil *Lotus pedunculatus*/Barra-mhìslean

Habitat: Common is very common on dry grasslands, machair and dunes. Greater is uncommon on wet grasslands and wet heath with recent records from West Coll only, not Tiree.

Common Bird's-foot-trefoil

Form: **sprawling**/weakly **erect** up to 25cm, (can reach 50cm).

Flowers: 10mm–16mm.

Leaves: **alternate**, **oval**, 3mm-10mm.

Fruit: 15mm-30mm, slender, straight **pods**.

Common Bird's-foot-trefoil's **flower-head** has two to seven bright yellow flowers, often tinged with red or orange. Its buds are red tipped and its stem is solid. Greater Bird's-foot-trefoil flowers are more often a clear yellow, only rarely tinged, and it usually has five to twelve flowers making up its **flower-head**. Its stem is hollow. Aside from the varying overall size and difference in habitat, these two can also be distinguished by the hairs on the leaves and stems of the Greater Bird's-foot-trefoil, whereas the Common is most often hairless. Despite their name (trefoil = three leaves), both plants actually have five leaflets; however, the two lower ones are attached to the stem like **stipules**. You will find Greater Bird's-foot-trefoil in damper places than the Common. The fruit of both are arranged in a bird's-foot shape. See also Kidney Vetch (page 93) and Meadow Vetchling (page 110).

The leaves of Common Bird's-foot-trefoil are food to the larvae of the Six-spot Burnet Moth on Coll and Gunna, although oddly this moth is absent from Tiree. For both plants, heavy insects, such as bees, reach the pollen by landing on and weighing down the lower two petals.

Greater Bird's-foot-trefoil

Form: **erect** up to 35mm, (can reach 60cm).

Flowers: 10mm–12mm.

Leaves: **alternate**, broadly **oval**, 15mm-20mm.

Fruit: 15mm-30mm, slender, straight **pods**.

Pea family

	Flowering:	Seeds:				
	May - Sep	Jun - Aug	Common			
	Jun - Aug	Jul - Aug	Greater			109

Meadow Vetchling *Lathyrus pratensis*/Peasair Bhuidhe

Habitat: common in grassy places throughout the islands, particularly in ditches and on roadsides.

This is the only yellow-flowered vetch on the islands that climbs through vegetation. The pea-like flowers are tightly clustered at the end of the long, angular stem. It climbs up through grasses and supports itself with fine curly **tendrils**, which are located at the final sets of paired leaflets. The **stipules** are **arrow shaped**, and the seed **pod** is long and black. The flowers are similar to Bird's-foot-trefoil (page 109), but that plant has **trifoliate** leaves and much looser clusters of flowers.

Form:	**trailing/climbing** up to 70cm, (can reach 100cm).
Flowers:	10mm-15mm long.
Leaves:	**alternate** pairs of **lance-shaped** leaflets, up to 5cm long.
Fruit:	**pod**, 2cm-4cm long.

The unusual angled stems, bearing slight wings, separate this species from all of the vetches.

Pea family

Flowering: Jun - Sep   Seeds: Aug - Sep

Marsh St. John's-wort *Hypericum elodes*/Meas an Tuirc Coille

Habitat: occasional by lochans, pools, and streams.

Marsh St. John's-wort is a less than typical St. John's-wort. The classic five yellow petals and bunches of red **stamens** are there but the flower does not open as fully as other species. The leaves are **opposite**, **untoothed** and stalkless, as with other St John's-worts (page 107), but they are more grey than green and are covered in velvety hairs. The upright stems are soft, greyish and conspicuously hairy and bear groups of yellow flowers, which are half closed. The **sepals** have red marginal dots. Marsh St. John's-wort tends to be found in out of the way places by boggy pools, where they creep almost un-noticed.

Form: **creeping** to **erect**, up to 30cm, (can reach 40cm).

Flowers: 15mm across.

Leaves: opposite, **circular** to **oval**.

Marsh St. John's-wort is the clan badge of the MacKinnons. The St. John's-wort family has a long history of medical use. The Latin name '*Hypericum*' is derived from Greek and means 'over an apparition', a reference to the belief that the herb would cause evil spirits to leave. Our terminology and understanding of illness may have evolved over the centuries, but St. John's-wort is still at the centre of a multi-million pound industry providing herbal anti-depressants.

St. John's-wort family

Bog Asphodel *Narthecium ossifragum*/Bliochan

Habitat: common and locally abundant on wet heath and bog.

Bog Asphodel can be strikingly abundant on the seemingly monochrome moors. The **raceme** consists of up to twenty individual flowers, so the plant can look as though it has only a single flower, or a colourful bunch of bright yellow, star-like flowers. Each flower consists of six yellow pointed petals and six orange **anthers** and the leaves are flattened in one plane. In autumn the whole plant turns a glorious orange colour. The fruit capsules resemble stars as they split into segments and the whole seed head looks like a small bottle brush.

Form:	**erect**, 5cm-20cm, (can reach 45cm).
Flowers:	10mm-15mm across.
Leaves:	mainly **basal**, **sword shaped**, 2cm-15cm long,
Fruit:	star shaped.

Bog Asphodel is sometimes called "bone-breaker" as the habitat it grows in is wet and lacking in calcium, so stock grazed exclusively in the areas - and by implication on this plant - can be prone to weak bones and foot rot. Bog Asphodel can also cause photosensitivity in sheep, probably due to chemicals called saponins.

Lily family

Flowering: Jul - Aug   Seeds: Aug - Oct

Biting Stonecrop *Sedum acre*/Gràbhan nan Clach

Habitat: frequent on machair.

Biting Stonecrop is a small, mat-forming, evergreen succulent plant, which grows in the machair and close to the sea. The **inflorescence** has two to three main branches, each with two to four bright yellow flowers. There are five petals and ten prominent **stamens**. The leaves are succulent, yellow-green in colour and are pressed to the stem.

Form: **creeping**, to 10cm.

Flowers: 12mm across

Leaves: rounded **oval**, 3mm-5mm long.

The name, Biting Stonecrop, arises from its hot and peppery taste. Two thousand years ago, Pliny, a Roman natural philosopher, recommended it as a means of procuring sleep, for which purpose he says it must be wrapped in a black cloth and placed under the pillow of the patient, without his knowing it, otherwise it will not be effective. Other herbalists recommended it for scurvy.

Stonecrop family

Flowering: Jun - Jul

Ribwort Plantain *Plantago lanceolata*/Slàn-lus

Habitat: widespread and abundant, particularly in grasslands.

Ribwort Plantain is the most widespread of the four plantain species that occur on the islands, although all are frequently seen. Members of the plantain family all have leaves in a **basal rosette**, with the **inflorescence** on tough, long, leafless stalks. The individual flowers are tiny, but have long, conspicuous **stamens**, making the **inflorescences** look like fluffy brushes. Ribwort Plantain has a deeply-furrowed, hairy stalk and leaves, with three to five prominent, parallel veins. Greater Plantain has broad, oval leaves and a much longer **inflorescence** on its unfurrowed stalk. Sea Plantain has narrow, fleshy leaves, a more linear **inflorescence** and an unfurrowed stalk. It is more restricted to salt marshes and coastal turf. Buck's-horn Plantain has deeply-divided, downy leaves, resembling deer antlers, whence it gets its name.

Form: **erect**, to 40cm.

Flowers: 2mm-4mm.

Leaves: **basal rosette**, **lance shaped**.

Children can play 'soldiers' with the **inflorescences**, in much the same way as 'conkers', where the opponent's head is knocked off. The juice from the leaves is good at staunching bleeding. These two facts are independent of one another!

Ribwort Plantain

Plantain family

Flowering: Apr - Oct

Sea Plantain

Greater Plantain

Buck's-horn Plantain

Bog-myrtle *Myrica gale*/Roid

Habitat: locally common on heath and bog, particularly on Coll.

Bog-myrtle is a substantial green shrub often overlooked amongst the heather. Brush against it, however, and the fragrance from the bruised leaves will identify it immediately. The **inflorescence** is either a male or female catkin (a condensed **spike** of reduced flowers). The red-brown male catkins are longer than the dark green female catkins which turn yellow with age. The grey-green leaves are wider towards the tip and have a downy underside.

Form: **erect** shrub, 50cm-100cm (can reach 150cm).

Flowers: 5mm or 10mm long.

Leaves: oblong, tapered at base, **toothed** at tip, 2cm-6cm long.

Bog-myrtle is a plant of many facets – no wonder it is the clan badge of the Campbells, lairds of Tiree. It can be used to flavour beer instead of using hops, and as a delicious herb with game dishes. Its bark is used to tan leather, to produce a yellow dye for tweed, and to make a candle wax. In places as diverse as the Hebrides, China, and North America it was used to cure ulcers.

For many years Coll Herbals has produced a midge repellent from Bog-myrtle, recently given as wedding favours at the editor's island wedding on Ballyhough Beach!

Bog-myrtle family

Flowering: Apr - May   Leaves only: Jun - Sep

Lesser Meadow-rue *Thalictrum minus*/Rù Beag

Habitat: frequent and widespread in dunes and machair.

Lesser Meadow-rue has an architectural quality to it, as it branches and zigzags up through spiky Marram leaves (page 121). The loose clusters of tiny yellow flowers are intriguing, as the petals are inconspicuous and the **sepals** are non-existent. On close examination, you see that it is the long yellow **stamens** that give the flowers their colour and shaggy appearance.

A red dye can be extracted from the roots.

Form: **erect** or spreading, up to 50cm (can reach 120cm).

Flowers: **inflorescence**, up to 10cm long.

Leaves: 3-4 times **pinnate** with small, lobed leaflets as broad as long.

leaves

Buttercup family

Tormentil *Potentilla erecta*/Cairt Lair

Habitat: widespread and frequent on the more acidic soils of cliffs and heathland.

A weak and slender plant of acidic soils, which grows up through the grass and is often supported by other vegetation. The bright yellow flowers have four slightly notched petals, and the gaps between these reveal the green **sepals** below in the form of a green cross. The leaves have three **oval** leaflets that are blunt **toothed** at the edge and bear two short **stipules** at the base. The flowers of the similar Silverweed (page 106) have five to six petals.

leaf

Form: **trailing**, 4cm-12cm (can reach 45cm).

Flowers: 7mm-15mm across.

Leaves: **pinnate** with **oval** leaflets, **toothed**, up to 16mm long.

Also known as Cinquefoil, which means "five leaved" in French – a reference to the three lobes plus two **stipules** on each leaf. The plant has many uses: when boiled in water, the roots release a thick red juice, which was used both for dying and for tanning leather and fishing nets; boiling in milk produced a medicine for the treatment of colic and other gastric complaints. In his book, *Off in a Boat*, Neil Gunn records a belief of Skye locals that Tormentil would grow up into a buttercup (Gunn 1990).

Rose family

Flowering: Jun - Sep

Groundsel *Senecio vulgaris*/Grunnasg

Habitat: widespread on fore-dunes, in gardens and in disturbed or waste ground.

This familiar yellow-flowered member of the daisy family is a type of ragwort and is characterised by its loose clusters of yellow, cylindrical **florets** atop an often hairy, reddish stem. The **flower-heads** are made up of 4mm long yellow **florets** and 6mm long narrow, black tipped, greenish **bracts**. It lacks the **ray florets**

of other ragworts. The leaves are hairless above but cottony below. The lower leaves are stalked and the upper leaves clasp the stem. The seeds are dispersed as small 'dandelion clocks'.

Form:	erect 20cm-40cm.
Flowers:	10mm long and 4mm across.
Leaves:	deeply cut into blunt, **oval**-oblong lobes.
Fruit:	dandelion-like clocks, 10mm-15mm across.

Groundsel is one of the commonest plants in Britain, but rarer on the islands. It is recorded as being used to treat horses for swellings and as a cure for rheumatism in humans.

Daisy family

Flowering: Apr - Oct   Leaves only: Mar   Seeds: Jul - Oct

Introduction to the green section

This section is small but dramatic. From the grand sweeps of the Marram grass in the dunes, to the tiny seeds of Fat–hen to the fleshy leaves of Babington's Orache, these green-flowering plants are steeped in the history of Scotland, with uses ranging from provision of shelter to food. The use of Marram in thatching is well known, and testifies to the resourcefulness of the islanders. With no money to purchase superior materials, the islanders looked around and used what was provided for them naturally within their environment. Green flowers are not particularly attractive to insects, so the scent becomes an important feature for survival.

Frog Orchid

Marram *Ammophila arenaria*/Muran

Habitat: abundant in the fore dunes.

Marram has a stout **flower-head**, like a spiky whitish-green cigar. The leaves are tough and rigid with sharp points. They are grey green and normally rolled into a half-cylinder. Marram is the backbone of the dune systems in the Hebrides. It is an extremely tough **perennial** grass that spreads by way of long underground stems, called **rhizomes**, which form mats that bind the sand. It plays a vital role in combating coastal erosion. Over-harvesting and poor management have caused many problems of sand-blow in the past, resulting in landlords on both islands introducing regulations for tenants to plant Marram wherever the dunes may be breached.

Form: **erect,** up to 120cm.

Flowers: **flower-head** up to 20cm long.

Leaves: **sword shaped**, up to 100cm.

Marram grass is such a tough and versatile material that it has been used extensively to make string, rope, mats, baskets, saddle blankets, bags and even hats and shoes. On Tiree, local craftsmen still cut Marram from the fore dunes to create the beautiful thatched houses. The Marram on Coll is also cut for use on Tiree.

Grass family

Flowering: Jul - Aug

121

Branched Bur-reed *Sparganium erectum*/Seisg Rìgh

Habitat: frequent by streams, ditches, lochs and pools.

Branched Bur-reed is a curious looking aquatic plant, with long, thin, green leaves, which are broadside on to the stem. The leaves are triangular in section. The flowers look like burrs. In fact, the flowers are tiny and are grouped into globular heads. The female flowers are in larger heads lower down the **inflorescence**, while the male flowers are crowded in smaller balls towards the top.

Form: **erect**, to 150cm.

Flowers: flower-heads, up to 3cm across.

Leaves: up to 150cm long, 2cm-3cm wide.

The Gaelic translates as 'King's sedge'.

Grass family

Flowering: Jun - Aug

Common Twayblade *Listera ovata*/Da-dhuilleach Coitcheann

Habitat: very local on machair.

The fifteen to thirty yellow-green flowers form a loose **raceme**, with individual flowers looking very much like a small man. The **dorsal petals** and **sepals** form a loose **hood** (the head); the blunt, oval **lateral sepals** are spread to the sides (the arms), and it has a long, forked **lip** (the legs). The stem is long, pale green and hairy. The two **basal** leaves are dark green with noticeable veins.

Form:	**erect,** 20cm-40cm, (can reach 75cm).
Flowers:	loose **raceme**, 7cm-25cm long.
Leaves:	**basal**, **opposite**, broad, **oval**.

The common name almost certainly comes from Old Norse for 'two leaves'. The life cycle (from germination to flowering) of this species can be up to fifteen years, although recent studies show it generally to be from two to three years.

Orchid family

Babington's Orache *Atriplex glabriuscula*/Praiseach Mhìn Cladaich

Habitat: frequent and widespread on sandy shores, more rarely on open ground away from the shore.

Babington's Orache is the most frequent and widespread of several similar, weedy-looking orache species, which occur at the tops of beaches. When in flower or fruit the plant is likely to appear more **erect**, otherwise it is **prostrate**. It has distinctive **spear-shaped** leaves with a broad base bearing pointed lobes and a pointed tip. The upper leaves are narrower. The plant is covered in mealy scales, which drop off as it matures and the entire plant can vary in colour from pale green to a reddish-mauve. The clusters of knobbly single-seeded fruit are surrounded by **bracts**. The fruits are more noticeable than the tiny inconspicuous flowers which are usually green.

Form: **erect** or **prostrate**, up to 50cm.

Flowers: 2mm across.

Leaves: **alternate**, **spear shaped**, up to 10cm across.

Fruit: 4mm-10mm, knobbly.

This plant is edible and was widely eaten on Tiree in the past. The Gaelic translates as 'smooth shore cabbage'.

Goosefoot family
Flowering: Jul - Sep   Leaves only: May - Jun   Seeds: Sep - Oct

Frog Orchid *Dactylorhiza viridis*/Mogairlean Losgainn

Habitat: widespread on dunes and machair.

The fifteen to thirty small, yellow-green to red-brown flowers form a compact **spike**. Some plants have copper-coloured flowers, whilst others are green, with both often growing side by side. The petals and **sepals** form a tight head-like **hood**, and it has a long, tongue-shaped, three-lobed **lip**. The central lobe is smaller and shorter than the two outer lobes and is slightly folded backwards. The **lip** is paler than the rest of the flower. The stem is green or coppery.

Form: **erect**, 5cm-15cm, (can reach 30cm).

Flowers: spike, 1cm-7cm long.

Leaves: **basal**, **oval**; stem leaves, **oval**, narrower towards **inflorescence**.

The individual flowers look (with a great deal of imagination) like a small frog.

Orchid family

Flowering: Jun - Aug

125

Fat-hen *Chenopodium album*/Càl Slapach

Habitat: widespread where ground is disturbed or cultivated.

Fat-hen is a large, robust plant of disturbed ground. Like othe members of the goosefoot family (e.g. Babington's Orache, pag 124), the leaves and stem are mealy. In this species, the stem often tinged with red, and has rather short, erect branches. It ha flowering **spike**s arising from the join of leaf and stem, with tin inconspicuous flowers, which have five **sepals** and no petals. Th fruits are the main distinguishing feature for each species in th family. These ripen in the autumn and are more noticeable ther Fat-hen has shallow, widely spaced furrows on its seed coat.

Form:	**erect** up to 100cm, (can reach 150cm).
Flowers:	2mm across.
Leaves:	lower leaves, **lance** to diamond shaped, bluntly **toothed**; upper leaves, **lance shaped**, usually untoothed.

Archaeological evidence suggests Fat-hen has been part of the Scottish di since prehistoric times. The young and tender plants are still eaten by Nativ Americans, and in Canada it is grown as animal fodder. The seeds can be eate raw, or made into a flour that is very similar to buckwheat. Hens love it too.

Goosefoot family

Flowering: Jul - Oct

Introduction to the white section

There are many small white flowers in this section that are difficult to identify. Don't get frustrated! Look upon this as the perfect opportunity to become more aware of the finer points of flower identification. You will need to increase your knowledge of flower anatomy, pay attention to the leaf shape and be sensitive to which type of habitat you are in, although the latter has no clear boundaries.

In early summer on Tiree, large areas of machair and in-bye fields are covered with thousands of Daisy blooms. These spectacular carpets of white again highlight the more extensive incursion of shell-sand across the island compared to Coll, thanks to Tiree's flatter nature and greater exposure to Atlantic gales. As a result, about a third of Tiree's land is influenced by the enriching properties of the shell-sand compared to around an eighth of Coll.

The identification of white flowers is further confused by the fact that some flowers, such as Sea Rocket (which is in the white section), can also appear in a lilac-pink form. Alternately, Water Lobelia usually appears as pale mauve so is in the blue-purple section of this book, but it can also have a white form!

Meadowsweet

White Water-lily *Nymphaea alba*/Duilleag-bhàite Bhàn

Habitat: frequent in acidic lochs of Central and NE Coll only.

This very striking and unmistakeable aquatic species has large floating leaves with a waxy upper surface. They are obvious through the summer, but die back in the winter. The stunning white, fragrant flowers grow on stalks just above the surface of the water. The flower has up to twenty- five petals, conspicuous yellow **stamens** and will only open fully in bright sunshine.

Form: erect.

Flowers: 9cm-20cm across.

Leaves: rounded, with a split almost to half way, 15cm-40cm across.

Fruit: globular, green and warty.

Red-throated Diver chicks sometimes secrete themselves in the mats of floating leaves. The roots were traditionally used in the Hebrides as a source of black or brown dye and were employed to treat corns when boiled in vinegar. More unusually, the roots were also said to 'allay lecherous dreams' (Milliken & Bridgewater 2004). It is known that Stone Age man ate the starchy roots, but the recent Ray Mears' television series failed to find a truly palatable manner in which to do this.

Water-lily family
Flowering: Jun - Sep   Leaves only: May - Oct   Seeds: Aug - Sep

Hogweed *Heracleum sphondylium*/Odharan
Wild Angelica *Angelica sylvestris*/Lus nam Buadh

Habitat: Hogweed is common and widespread in ditches, field margins and around habitation. Wild Angelica is common in marshes, ditches and on cliffs.

Hogweed

Form:	**erect,** 50cm-300cm.
Flowers: umbels,	5cm-20cm across.
Leaves:	**pinnate** with coarse-toothed, deeply-lobed leaflets.
Fruit:	flattened oval, up to 8mm long with two wings.

These two **umbellifers** are superficially similar, but differ in a number of ways, including habitat, shape of the **flower-head** and leaf shape. Hogweed prefers dry conditions and is typically seen in field margins and waste ground, where the most obvious identification feature is the flat, plate-like **umbels** (up to forty per plant) held at different levels. Although Wild Angelica will also be seen in damper field margins, it is much less frequent here. Wild Angelica has very obvious inflated sheaths linking the leaves to the stem which is usually hairless, hollow and often purplish. Hogweed has hairy, hollow, ridged stems. The leaflets of Wild Angelica are **oval** to **tear-drop shaped**, while those of Hogweed are rough, with raggedy lobes. See also Cow Parsley and Wild Carrot (page 132) and Pignut (page 133).

Wild Angelica

Form:	**erect,** 50cm-150cm.
Flowers: umbels,	3cm-15cm across.
Leaves:	3 times **pinnate** with **toothed, oval** to **tear-shaped** leaflets.
Fruit:	flattened egg-shape, up to 8mm long with four broad wings

Hogweed: Flowering: Jun - Oct   Leaves only: Apr - May   Carrot family

Wild Angelica: Flowering: Jun - Sep   Leaves only: Apr - May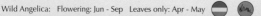

Parsley Water-dropwort *Oenanthe lachenalii*/Dàtha Bàn Peirsill

Habitat: locally common in salt marshes and marshy places.

Parsley Water-dropwort is a small **umbellifer** that grows in wet, particularly coastal areas. The open, convex **umbel** consists of many tiny, white flowers about two millimetres long. The leaflets are very thin. The seed is reddish, which distinguishes it from other water-dropworts, whose fruits are green.

Form: **erect**, to 80cm, (can reach 100cm).

Flowers: **umbels** 2cm-6cm wide.

Leaves: twice **pinnate**, with thin narrow leaflets.

Fruit: ovoid and reddish.

Parsley Water-dropwort is poisonous. However, it is the closely related Hemlock Water-dropwort that has been responsible for more fatalities than any other British vascular plant. Hemlock Water-dropwort, *Oenanthe crocata*, has been recorded from only nine places on the islands recently. Animals have learnt to avoid it, and so should you!

Carrot family

Flowering: Jun - Sep

Meadowsweet *Filipendula ulmaria*/Cneas Chù Chulainn

Habitat: common and widespread in wet grasslands and wetlands.

Over time, the individual, tiny flowers come into bloom. Once they are all out, they make a large, frothy, branching plume that smells of almonds, honey and high summer. With five upturned petals, five downturned **sepals** and many long **stamens**, the massed blooms of the Meadowsweet are a true delight. The leaves are dark green and hairless above, pale green and downy below. The plant bears clusters of six to ten spirally twisted, green fruits. From a distance, Meadowsweet can look similar to umbellifers such as Cow Parsley (page 132) or Hogweed (page 129), but the smell alone makes it easily distinguishable, and it does not have the 'flat head' so characteristic of the umbellifers.

Form: **erect**, up to 120cm.

Flowers: 4mm-10mm across.

Leaves: **pinnate**, 30cm-60cm long, with 2-5 pairs of sharp-**toothed** leaflets, 4cm-8cm long.

Fruit: round.

There are tantalising clues in the Hebrides that Meadowsweet was used in meads and ales from about two thousand years ago. This tradition continues with a commercially-produced beer, utilising Meadowsweet flowers, which is brewed in Scotland.

Rose family

Flowering: Jun - Sep   Seeds: Aug - Nov

Cow Parsley *Anthriscus sylvestris*/Costag Fhiadhain

Habitat: common in field margins and around habitation.

Cow Parsley is a tall, downy, herbaceous **umbellifer** with hollow, ridged and unspotted stems that frequently become purple with age. It can be mistaken for Wild Carrot (opposite), Hogweed or Wild Angelica (page 129), but as with all **umbellifers**, the fruit is the diagnostic feature. Cow Parsley fruits are green, slender and ridged, becoming black when ripe. The flowers of Cow Parsley have five petals and the **umbel** is **bract**less. The leaves are a fresh green and are slightly downy. Another similar plant is Pignut, but this plant is generally smaller and has much-divided leaves, recalling those of Dill.

Form: **erect**, up to 100cm, (can reach 150cm).

Flowers: umbels, 2cm-6cm across.

Leaves: 2-3 times **pinnate**, with fern-like leaflets.

Fruit: ridged, 6mm-10mm long and 1mm wide.

Is often planted as early-cover for corncrakes by the RSPB due to its vigorous growth early in the season. In Scottish superstition has been considered as one of the Devil's plants. Depending upon the fixing agent employed, Cow Parsley has been used to produce yellow, orange and green dyes.

Carrot family
Flowering: Apr - Jul   Leaves only: Feb - Mar, Sep, Oct   Seeds: Jun - Aug

Wild Carrot *Daucus carota* subsp. *carota* /Curran Fiadhain

Habitat: common in dune and machair grasslands.

Wild Carrot is an upright or spreading, hairy **umbellifer**, with long stalks and a strong, ridged stem. As with Cow Parsley (opposite), it may be confused with Hogweed or Wild Angelica (page 129). The fruit is the diagnostic feature. Wild Carrot fruits are oval and hairy with hooked spines. Its flowers are even smaller than those of

Cow Parsley and it has large, much-divided **bracts** beneath its concave **umbel**. Although the flowers of Wild Carrot are white, they can appear pinkish in bud and often have a characteristic purple/red flower in the centre of the **inflorescence**. When the grey-green leaves of Wild Carrot are crushed, they give off a strong carroty scent.

Form:	**erect** or spreading, up to 75cm.
Flowers:	**umbel,** 3cm-7cm across.
Leaves:	3 times **pinnate,** with leaflets deeply cut into narrow lobes.
Fruit:	oval, with hooked spines.

It is thought that some of the dwarf specimens from the Ben Feall area of Coll can be attributed to the subsp. *gummifer*, otherwise known as Sea Carrot, which has stouter, more succulent, stems, darker green leaves and saucer-shaped fruiting **umbels**. As the wild ancestor of the domestic carrot, its roots have been used for food, and although they are smaller and tougher than modern cultivated counterparts, they are actually much more aromatic. Wild Carrot might be the legendary *torranan*, a plant of great magical significance to the Hebridean crofter, whose primary function was to ensure a good supply of milk. It was used as a diuretic, especially against gout, in the Uists.

Carrot family

Yarrow *Achillea millefolium*/Eàrr-thalmainn
Sneezewort *Achillea ptarmica*/Cruaidh-lus

Habitat: Yarrow is very common in a wide range of grassland habitats. Sneezewort is occasional in ditches and wet grassland.

Yarrow

Form:	**erect**, up to 40cm, (can reach 80cm).
Flowers:	4mm-6mm across.
Leaves:	**alternate**, feathery, up to 15cm long.

The flowers of these two closely related species are superficially similar, but are easily distinguished. Yarrow has many white - or sometimes pink - flowers, gathered in tight flat-topped clusters. Sneezewort flowers are large, more daisy like in shape, with white petals gathered around a greenish-white central disc, and they occur in looser clusters. The **anthers** of Yarrow are yellow, but quickly turn brown, giving the flower a dirty appearance. Its leaves appear feathery, being divided into many fine segments, and they have a strong pungent smell when crushed. In contrast, the **lance-shaped** leaves of Sneezewort are scentless.

The pungent leaves of Yarrow were formerly used to flavour liqueurs. It is also very drought resistant, and the leaves remain fresh and green, long after grass has wilted during hot spells.

Sneezewort

Form:	**erect**, up to 60cm.
Flowers:	**flower-head**, up to 20mm across.
Leaves:	**alternate**, **lance shaped**, finely **toothed**, up to 6cm long.

Daisy family

  Yarrow

   Sneezewort

134

Flowering: Jul - Oct   Leaves only: Jun

Lesser Butterfly-orchid *Platanthera bifolia/*
Mogairlean an Dealain-dè Beag

Habitat: widespread, but local, in wet, heathy grassland.

This species often grows in groups of plants. Its characteristic 'butterfly-like' white flowers form a compact, cylindrical **spike**, making identification relatively easy. The spike consists of five to twenty-five flowers, each with a long narrow **lip** and a long **spur**. When viewed head-on, it can be seen that the **pollinia** (a mass of pollen grains which have stuck together within the **anther**) are parallel. In addition to the pair of fleshy **basal** leaves, there are several scale-like leaves sheathing the rounded stem. This species has a very strong scent of vanilla. The only truly similar species is the Greater Butterfly-orchid, which is larger in all aspects, and in which the greenish **lip** is much longer, and the **pollinia** diverge. However, there are only one or two recent records of that species on the islands, on the moorland of Tiree. It could also be confused with Irish Lady's-tresses (page 136), but other than both having white flowers, the two are very different.

Form: **erect**, 15cm-30cm.

Flowers: 11mm-18mm across.

Leaves: basal pair, large and **oval.**

In the years between 1964 and 2002, there has been a 33% decline, UK wide, in Lesser Butterfly-orchid, mainly due to the drainage of fields, the ploughing up of grassland and heath, the use of fertilizers and herbicides, and heavy summer grazing. It is one of a select group of species chosen for special attention under Scottish Natural Heritage's Species Action Framework.

Orchid family

Irish Lady's-tresses *Spiranthes romanzoffiana*/Mogairlean Bachlan ▶

Habitat: rare and local in nutrient-poor, wet-flushed grassland, at around 30 sites on Coll and two sites on Tiree.

The **inflorescence** has up to twenty creamy white flowers which occur in three distinct, twisted rows and give off a scent similar to Hawthorn flowers. If you can find one, this orchid is one of the easiest to identify, but the number that actually produce flowers each year varies considerably. The tubular flowers are formed by the strap-like **petals**, triangular **sepals** and the base of the **lip**. The tip of the **lip** protrudes downwards like a small tongue and is lightly green-veined. The stem is apple-green with downy hairs towards the tip. The leaves are yellow-green, with edges slightly rolled inwards. Stem leaves are sheathing.

Form: **erect**, 10cm-20cm, (can reach 30cm).

Flowers: inflorescence, 2cm-5cm long.

Leaves: **linear** to **lance shaped**.

The first Scottish record of this essentially North American orchid came from Coll in 1921. There is strong evidence that it flowers best following winter trampling by cattle. One of the sites on Tiree was only found in 2007 – there may be more out there to be discovered.

Orchid family

Flowering: Aug - Sep   Leaves only: Jul

Large Bindweed *Calystegia silvatica*/Dùil Mhial Mhòr

Habitat: a rare but increasing weed of roadsides and gardens in West Tiree, no recent records from Coll.

Large Bindweed has large attractive **trumpet-like** flowers in which the petals are fused together. These are entirely white, bearing two overlapping green **bracts** beneath. The long, tough, twisting stems wind around other plants and objects close to the ground, often smothering plants in the process. The leaves are notched at the base, but are larger than those of Sea Bindweed (page53), are not fleshy and are more pointedly **arrow shaped**.

Form: **climbing/sprawling**, up to 3m, (can reach 5m).

Flowers: generally less than 70mm across (can reach 90mm)

Leaves: **arrow shaped**, up to 10cm long.

Large Bindweed is an aggressive weed, which has been introduced to Britain from southern Europe.

Bindweed family

Daisy *Bellis perennis*/Neòinean
Oxeye Daisy *Leucanthemum vulgare*/Neòinean Mòr

Habitat: Daisy is abundant in grassland and machair; Oxeye Daisy is locally frequent in similar places.

Daisy

Form: **erect**, up to 10cm, (can reach 12cm).

Flowers: 2cm wide.

Leaves: basal rosette, spoon shaped.

Few plants are more recognisable than the diminutive Daisy, and its larger cousin, the Oxeye Daisy. Both have yellow inner **disc florets** and white outer **ray florets**. Although size is the easiest distinguishing difference, Daisies have pink tips to the petals, colouring the fields pink as the petals close at night. Oxeye Daisies always have white petals. The **basal** leaves of the Oxeye are slightly tougher, darker green, and have wavier edges and it has stalkless stem leaves. The Daisy has no stem leaves.

The Daisy embeds itself in our culture with the making of daisy chains, and the plucking of petals to the refrain of "she loves me, she loves me not". Both types of Daisy once had a reputation as a good cure for fresh wounds, and were often called Bruisewort. It is still used today in homeopathic medicine.

Oxeye Daisy

Form: **erect**, up to 50cm, (can reach 75cm).

Flowers: 5cm wide.

Leaves: basal rosette, spoon shaped; stem leaves, deeply **toothed**.

Daisy family

138

Flowering: Daisy, Mar - Oct   Oxeye Daisy, May - Aug

Sea Mayweed *Tripleurospermum maritimum*/Buidheag na Mara

Habitat: common along the strandline of beaches.

A variable plant with large, daisy-like flowers that can be found growing around piles of old seaweed at the top of beaches. The **flower-heads** form a loose straggly group, with spreading, white, outer **ray florets** and yellow, inner **disc florets**. The leaves are like capillaries with cylindrical and fleshy leaflets. Scentless Mayweed is similar, but with more thread-like leaves, and grows inland, on disturbed ground.

Form: **erect** or **sprawling**, up to 50cm.

Flowers: **flower-head**, 2cm-4cm across.

Leaves: 2-3 times **pinnate** with narrow, blunt, cylindrical leaflets.

The daisy family has many similar looking flowers, and Ox-eye Daisy (opposite) has been confused with Sea Mayweed. Chamomile is also similar, and confusing that gentle herb with Sea Mayweed has led to unpleasant and acrid herb teas that have been responsible for causing allergies.

Daisy family

Common Cottongrass *Eriophorum angustifolium*/Canach
Hare's-tail Cottongrass *Eriophorum vaginatum*/Sìoda Monai

Habitat: common on peaty heaths and boggy pools.

Common Cottongrass

Form: **erect**, up to 40cm (can reach 60cm)

Flowers: 2cm-3cm long.

Leaves: grass like, up to 20cm long, less than 6mm wide.

Cottongrass, with its pure white cottony tufts of flowers dancing over the heathland in spring, is irresistibly heart-warming and joyful. The two species are easily distinguished as the Common Cottongrass has several blooms on each stem, with leaves that are v-shaped in section. The Hare's-tail Cottongrass has only one flower per stem, flowers earlier in the spring, and has thinner leaves, which are triangular in section. Hair's-tail Cottongrass forms tussocks, whilst the stems of Common Cottongrass are separate from each other.

Hare's-tail Cottongrass

Form: **erect**, up to 40cm (can reach 50cm)

Flowers: 2cm-3cm long.

Leaves: grass like, up to 20cm long, less than 6mm wide.

Cottongrasses, sometimes known as Bog Cotton, have been used to stuff pillows and mattresses. They are actually sedges, and keen botanists can find books on grasses and sedges that will hone their identification skills. The Gaelic name for Hare's-tail Cottongrass captures the feeling of the flower: 'moor silk'.

Sedge family

Flowering: Hare's-tail, Apr - May   Common, Jun - Jul

Bogbean *Menyanthes trifoliata*/Trì-bhileach

Habitat: widespread and frequent in marshes, ditches and at lochsides.

Bogbean grows up out of the water in wetlands and forms thick swathes at the edges of lochs and pools. The fleshy leaves are comprised of three **oval** leaflets with a rounded tip. The numerous pink buds are clustered towards the top of the stem and open to form a spectacular display of five-petalled white flowers. Each flower is fringed with long, thick, white hairs giving the plant its distinctive fluffy appearance.

Form: **erect** up to 35cm, (can reach 150cm).

Flowers: 15mm across.

Leaves: **trifoliate**, with **oval** leaflets, rounded tip, up to 12cm long,

Fruit: egg-shaped **cap-sule**; splits in two when ripe.

The leaves were once dried and made into tea as a cure for scurvy. Bogbean leaves were also used instead of hops in beer-making.

Bogbean family

Burnet Rose *Rosa pimpinellifolia*/Ròs Beag Bàn na h-Alba

Habitat: local on dunes and rocky outcrops.

This is a low shrub with stems and suckers forming extensive bushy patches in clumps. The stems are covered with straight, purplish thorns and numerous stiff bristles. Long before flowering, this species is conspicuous in the way that sheep's wool often adorns its thorny stems. The flower is typically rose-shaped, with the five creamy-white petals providing a sharp contrast to the plethora of golden-yellow **stamens**. The fruit is purplish black when ripe, and the undivided **sepals** often persist after the fruit has gone. Other species of wild rose, including Dog-rose, can be seen on the islands. Some of these have pink flowers.

Form:	**erect**, 20cm-40cm.
Flowers:	3cm-4cm across.
Leaves:	**pinnate**, with 7-11 **tear-drop-shaped** leaflets, 5mm-15mm long.
Fruit:	round, 15mm-30mm across.

The Burnet Rose, often called Scotch Rose, is thought to be the most likely candidate for the rose that Bonnie Prince Charlie pinned to his bonnet and later became the White Cockade of the Jacobites. Syrups and jams made from the hips of this species are said to be particularly pleasant.

Rose family

Flowering: Jun - Aug   Leaves only: May - Jun   Seeds: Jul - Aug

Bramble *Rubus fruticosus*/Dris

Habitat: scarce on Tiree, but locally common on Coll where grazing
pressure is low, such as cliffs, rock outcrops, road verges and
garden edges.

The bramble is an astonishing plant, growing long, arching,
spine-covered stems so fast you can almost see them move. Its
bushy briars of suckering stems are all we need to see to know
the reputation of this plant. The
flowers, with five petals and five
sepals, are quite large and can
vary from white to deep pink.
The fruit, green, then red, then
shiny black or purple, can be
delicious for birds, animals and
people.

Form:	scrambling, to 3m.
Flowers:	2cm-4cm across.
Leaves:	**palmate**, with 3-5 **oval** leaflets.

fruit

stem

The Bramble is one of those plants intimately
linked with human history. Mentioned in the Old
Testament, by the ancient Greeks, and by the earliest
herbalists, it is a plant of ritual, of food, of drink, of
medicine, of hooks and other practical materials. Today on the
islands it is still one of the most coveted of the wild plants. The
fruits, known as brambles or blackberries, freeze well, particularly
if spread out on a tray initially.

Rose family

Sea Campion *Silene uniflora*/Coirean na Mara

Habitat: occasional and local on coastal rocks, cliffs and dunes, including the steep sea cliffs at Ceann a' Mhara, Tiree.

Both campions have attractive flowers bearing five petals that are deeply notched; those of Sea Campion are white, whereas those of Red Campion (page 66) are deep pink. Sea Campion also has obvious greenish 'bladders', veined red beneath the flowers, which Red Campion lacks. Both species have flask-shaped seed capsules in autumn. The small leaves of Sea Campion are narrow and taper at either end. They are **glaucous** and slightly fleshy.

Sea Campion was variously known as 'Dead Man's Bells' or 'Devil's Hatties' and superstition forbade it to be picked or brought into the house. These ominous nicknames may have been associated with its presence on steep sea cliffs and rock ledges, in an attempt to discourage children from climbing on dangerous cliffs.

Form: **trailing** to **erect**, up to 30cm.

Flowers: 15mm-20mm across.

Leaves: **opposite**, **oval**, up to 6cm long.

Pink family

144

Flowering: May - Aug   Seeds: Sep

Grass-of-Parnassus *Parnassia palustris*/Fionnan Geal

Habitat: locally frequent in wet grassland particularly in wet hollows in dunes, more rarely on heath land and dry machair. Largely restricted to the Reef on Tiree, more widespread and frequent on Coll, where it is particularly noticeable on damp roadside verges.

The solitary, delicate and rather beautiful flowers are raised on slender stalks, each comprising five white petals bearing greenish veins. Within the flower, the five green **stamens** are surrounded by an unusual arrangement of feathery, yellow staminodes (sterile stamens) which unfold, one at a time, throughout the day. The staminodes exude a glistening yellow liquid, to which insects are attracted, falsely believing it to be nectar. There is normally a small single leaf clasping the flower stem.

Form: **erect**, up to 15cm, (can reach 30cm).

Flowers: 15mm-30mm across.

Leaves: **basal**, **heart shaped**, up to 5cm long,

A member of the saxifrage family and not a grass at all, the unusual name links the pretty flowers with the grass of the holy mountain of Apollo and the Muses. An infusion of the leaves was once used to settle the stomach as well as to treat liver and nervous complaints.

Saxifrage family

White Clover *Trifolium repens*/Seamrag Bhàn

Habitat: widespread and often very common in most habitats.

This flower is found in most habitats, and is often sown in grass seed mixes. The round, scented **flower-heads** are composed of forty to eighty, small, individual flowers. As the plant goes over, the lower flowers can droop down as they turn from creamy white (sometimes tinged pale pink) to brown. The leaflets are often marked with a white V-shape.

Form: **creeping** to **erect**, to 20cm, (can reach 50cm).

Flowers: flower-head, 1cm-3cm across; individual flowers, 7mm-10mm.

Leaves: pinnate with 3 **circular toothed** leaflets.

leaf

White Clover is the clan badge of the Sinclair family. As well as being a nitrogen- fixing plant, it shares other useful properties with Red Clover (page 68). White Clover has been used in the treatment of gastritis, enteritis, severe diarrhoea and rheumatic pains, as it possesses astringent, anti-inflammatory and antiseptic properties. The Gaelic translates as 'white shamrock'

Pea family

Flowering: Jun - Sep

Sea Rocket *Cakile maritima/Fearsaideag*

Habitat: locally common at the top of sandy beaches and occasional in salt marshes.

Sea Rocket is an attractive and striking plant that can grow in large numbers along the top of some of the most exposed sandy beaches on the islands, where it is a 'pioneer'. The flowers are white or lilac-pink, with four petals, and appear in short **racemes**. The leaves are succulent and shiny and can be so deeply **toothed** that they seem to comprise of leaflets. Thus, this simple leaf can

be described as **pinnate-toothed**. It has a long tap root and this, along with the fleshy leaves, allow it to seek out and retain moisture.

Form: **sprawling** to **erect**, up to 25cm.

Flowers: 6mm-12mm across.

Leaves: simple to **pinnate-toothed**, **linear** to oblong.

The plant, and its fruit segments, containing the seeds, will be washed away by the winter storms. Despite their dispersal by the sea water, the seeds do not lose their viability and they go on to colonise new spots. The salt in the sea water inhibits germination until rain washes it out. Some of the seeds will also have been buried at the high tide mark, ready to germinate there in the coming year.

Cabbage family

Water-cress *Rorippa nasturtium-aquaticum*/Biolair Uisge

Habitat: common in streams and ditches, especially near the coast.

Water-cress can be found growing thickly in some streams, often covering the water. The hollow, dark-green to purple stems creep and root below the surface, while flowering shoots float or rise up, bearing groups of small, white flowers. The petals are twice as long as the **sepals**. The leaves are dark green, comprising a ladder of **oval** leaflets, with a larger, rounder leaflet at the top.

Form:	**creeping** to **erect**, 10cm-60cm, (can reach 100cm.
Flowers:	4mm-6mm across.
Leaves:	**pinnate**, with **alternate**, **oval** leaflets.

Water-cress is very nutritious, and is grown and harvested throughout the UK. The sharp taste is particularly good in salads. However, if you harvest from the wild, beware of liver fluke: a parasitic worm that lives in a snail that can be found on Water-cress.

Cabbage family

Flowering: May - Sep

Thread-leaved Water-crowfoot
Ranunculus trichophyllus/Lìon na h-Aibhne

Lesser Water-plantain
Baldellia ranunculoides/Corr-chopag Bheag

Habitat: Lesser Water-plantain is nationally a rather rare aquatic plant, although locally frequent on Coll and Tiree.

Thread-leaved Water-crowfoot

Form: aquatic and submerged.

Flowers: 5mm-15mm.

Leaves: finely divided, like capillaries.

Thread-leaved Water-crowfoot is a buttercup with white flowers and a yellow base to the petal. It grows underwater and is sometime left high and dry on the mud of small pools. The leaves of Thread-leaved Water-crowfoot are very finely divided. Lesser Water-plantain is a rare aquatic plant, pleasantly frequent here. It is a member of the water-plantain family and has pale pink flowers with three petals, which are either held in a simple **umbel**, or appear in two **whorls**. The leaves taper into long stalks and smell of coriander. Although mostly **basal**, they can appear in **whorls** on the stem.

Lesser Water-plantain roots smell strongly of rotting eggs!

Lesser Water-plantain

Form: **erect**, to 20cm.

Flowers: 10mm-15mm.

Leaves: mostly **basal**, **lance shaped**.

Water-crowfoot: buttercup family   Water-plantain: water-plantain family
Lesser Water-plantain

Mountain Everlasting *Antennaria dioica*/Spòg Cait

Habitat: occasional on dry rocky habitats.

Usually found sprouting from short turf on rocky mounds, Mountain Everlasting is a super wee plant that is easily overlooked. The flower stem is white felted, as is the underside of the leaves. Male and female flowers appear on separate plants. The male flower has petal-like **bracts** enclosing the **flower-head**, which is smaller (six millimetres) than the female (twelve millimetres). The female flower also has papery **bracts**, but they are much narrower. There can be up to ten **flower-heads** grouped at the end of the stem, with tiny, individual **florets**. Males tend to be white, while females are tinged pink.

Form: **creeping** and **erect** to 10cm, (can reach 20cm).

Flowers: flower-heads, 5mm-12mm across.

Leaves: basal rosette, **oval** to **spoon shaped**; stem leaves more pointed.

Sometimes known as the Scottish Edelweiss, Mountain Everlasting has been used by herbalists for its astringent properties to treat such diverse ailments as diarrhoea, snake-bite, and mumps. The Gaelic translates as 'cat's paw', perhaps in relation to the felted feel of the stem and arrangement of the flowers.

Daisy family

Flowering: Jun - Jul

Shepherd's-purse *Capsella bursa-pastoris*/An Sporan

Habitat: common on waste ground and as an arable plant.

This distinctive and familiar annual plant of disturbed ground is actually a member of the cabbage family. The small flowers appear in terminal clusters, and of the four white petals, two are much shorter than the others. The green, heart-shaped, flattened fruit, which give this plant its name, form at the end of long, thin stems, which emerge from the - sometimes hairy - main stem. The upper leaves clasp the stem and are normally hairy.

Form: **erect**, 10cm-35cm.

Flowers: 2mm-3mm across.

Leaves: **basal rosette**, deeply lobed to undivided; stem leaves, **toothed**, **sword-shaped**, with pointed **basal** lobes.

The Gaelic translates as 'the purse'. This plant was formerly used in Scotland to treat haemorrhaging during child birth. The seeds were used by the Apache for making a bread flour.

Cabbage family

English Stonecrop *Sedum anglicum*/Biadh an t-Sionnaidh

Habitat: frequent in short turf and on rocks.

English Stonecrop is a small, succulent evergreen plant, usually **glaucous**, but often tinged red. It creeps and forms mats, often on bare rock crevices, or almost hidden in the machair. In summer it suddenly becomes more noticeable, as it produces two or three flowering stems. Each stem has three to six star-like, white flowers, which are pink-tinged on the back of the petals. The leaves are succulent and overlap each other in a spiral up the stem.

Form: **creeping**, to 5cm tall, (can reach 10cm).

Flowers: 12mm across.

Leaves: rounded **oval**, 3mm-5mm long.

The leaves and stalks have been crushed and used as a cooling plaster for many kinds of inflammation. It has also been eaten as a pickle. The Gaelic translates as 'food of the Prince'.

Stonecrop family

Flowering: Jun - Sep

Common Scurvygrass *Cochlearia officinalis*/Am Maraiche
Danish Scurvygrass *Cochlearia danica*/Carran Danmhairceach

Habitat: widespread and common near the coast.

Common Scurvygrass

Form: **erect** 5cm-50cm.

Flowers: 8mm-10mm across.

Leaves: **basal rosette, kidney** or **heart shaped**; stem leaves, triangular.

Common and Danish Scurvygrass are classic maritime plants, found on rocks, beaches, salt marshes and grassy habitats near the sea. The leaves are distinctively fleshy, with **basal** leaves appearing on long stalks. The two species can be distinguished by looking at the stalkless, clasping, triangular stem leaves of Common Scurvygrass, compared with the stalked, ivy-shaped lower stem leaves of Danish Scurvygrass. The small, white flowers on the flowering stalk quickly mature into swollen seed **pods**. The flowers of Danish Scurvygrass are usually pink and smaller and appear much earlier in the year. The fruits have more pointed ends than the rounded fruit of the Common Scurvygrass.

Common Scurvygrass is rich in vitamin C, and has been used to treat and prevent scurvy since ancient times. The Gaelic translates as 'the sailor'.

Danish Scurvygrass

Form: **erect** 10cm-20cm, (can reach 25cm).

Flowers: 4mm-5mm across.

Leaves: **basal rosette, heart shaped**; lower stem leaves, ivy shaped.

Cabbage family

Eyebright *Euphrasia nemorosa*/Lus nan Leac

Habitat: common in coastal grassland, on machair and also on knolls.

The flowers of Eyebright have a longer lower than upper **lip**. The petals form a whitish-pink, lobed **tube** with purple lines and a yellow throat blotch. The leaves are often bronze tinged. Eyebrights are short, annual, semi-parasitic herbs with almost orchid-like flowers. Their roots extract nutrients from grass roots. They form a very variable group, which excites controversy among botanical taxonomists. Some argue that there are more than a dozen closely related species on Coll and Tiree, with more than a hundred nationally. Like dandelions and brambles, eyebrights are easy on the eye, but beware getting involved in the tricky business of species identification!

Form: **erect**, 2cm-15cm, (can reach up to 35cm).

Flowers: 5mm-8mm long.

Leaves: **opposite**, **oval** to **circular**, deeply **toothed**, 5mm-10mm long.

leaf

Figwort family

Flowering: Jun - Sep

Eyebright *Euphrasia heslop-harrisonii*/Lus nan Leac

Habitat: rare at two salt marsh locations on Coll.

Distinguishing between the different species of eyebright is notoriously difficult. The most abundant forms on the islands are the machair and grassland species, *Euphrasia micrantha* and *Euphrasia nemerosa* (opposite), and the moorland variety *Euphrasia scottica*. Several others have been recorded on Coll and Tiree, with the salt marsh species, *Euphrasia heslop-harrisonii*, being one of the real Coll specialties. The combination of its specialised habitat and its very small form provide some assistance with identification, but the main feature to study of *Euphrasia heslop-harrisonii* is the shape of the fleshy leaves, in particular the **basal** teeth of the leaves, which curve upwards and outwards whilst the **basal** teeth of *nemorosa* stick out almost at right angles.

Form: **erect**, 4cm-8cm, (can reach 15cm).

Flowers: 4mm-6mm long.

Leaves: **opposite**, **oval**, **toothed**, 5mm-7mm long.

Endemic to Scotland. The eyebright species are under discussion, and there is not, as yet, a specific common or Gaelic name for the *heslop-harrisonnii*. Eyebrights, as their name implies, have been - and are still - used as a common and effective treatment for eye complaints. The latin name, *Euphrasia* comes from Euphrosyne, who was one of the three Graces of Greek history. The name means gladness, and Euphrosyne was renowned for her joyfulness. It is thought that the plant was named after her as its healing powers bring great gladness to those suffering from eye complaints.

Flowering: Jul - Sep

Figwort family

Common Mouse-ear *Cerastium fontanum*/Cluas luch Choitchear

Habitat: very common on sandy soils.

Common Mouse-ear is a very common plant, similar to and related to Common Chickweed (page 167) and Bog Stitchwort. The small flowers have five white petals, which are deeply notched and are slightly longer than the green **sepals**; unlike those of Bog Stitchwort and Common Chickweed, which have petals shorter than the **sepals**. The flowers arise on branching stalks from the junctions of the pairs of leaves. The stems and leaves are covered in small, white hairs. There are several closely related mouse-ears which also occur on these islands. Sea Mouse-ear has minute glands on the tiny hairs covering it, and no silver margins to the **bracts**. Sticky Mouse-ear also has glandular hairs, but is a little bigger, with flowers in a denser head.

Form:	**creeping** and ascending to 40cm.
Flowers:	3mm-12mm across.
Leaves:	paired, **oval** to **tear-drop shaped**, hairy, 1cm-3cm long.

This is one of the fifty commonest plants in Britain.

Pink family

Flowering: Apr - Oct

Sea Sandwort *Honckenya peploides*/Lus a' Ghoill

Habitat: common on sandy beaches and in salt marshes.

A very hardy seashore plant that conserves moisture in its succulent leaves. The Gaelic literally translates as plant of the 'hanging lip' or 'shield'.

A very short, salt-tolerant plant, which can form large mats on the upper edges of sandy beaches, often close to the tide-line. The succulent, yellowy-green oval leaves are stalkless and **opposite**, occurring in two rows at right angles up the stem. The tiny flowers have five spaced **sepals** and five shorter petals, but are the same green as the leaves and are easily missed. Much more distinctive are the rounded, yellow-green fruit **capsules**. Biting Stonecrop (page 113) has similar leaves, but these are much smaller than those of Sea Sandwort and turn red with age. It lacks the distinctive rounded fruits and bears bright yellow flowers.

Form: hugs ground in mats, 4cm-12cm (can reach 25cm).

Flowers: up to 10mm across.

Leaves: opposite, **oval**, up to 15mm long.

Fruit: up to 20mm across, spherical.

Pink family

Knotgrass *Polygonum aviculare*/Glùineach Bheag

Habitat: scarce in trampled ground.

Four species of knotgrass can be found on the islands. Knotgrass, Equal-leaved Knotgrass, and Northern Knotgrass occur as mat-forming plants in potato fields and other disturbed or cultivated areas, whilst the fourth, Ray's Knotgrass, is restricted to sandy beaches. The stem of Knotgrass can have swollen joints and the leaves are **alternate** and stalkless, with silvery and fringed scales at their base. The leaves are shorter on the flowering stem than the main stem. Knotgrass flowers can be white to pink and grow in the angle between the leaf and the stem. The closely related Northern Knotgrass, which occurs on Tiree, not Coll, has **oval** leaves and a larger fruit, whilst Equal-leaved Knotgrass has short, blunt leaves that are nearly all of equal length. Ray's Knotgrass has larger flowers, slightly turned back edges to the leaves and black seeds later in the year.

Form:	**prostrate**, sometimes **erect**, up to 100cm, (can reach 200cm).
Flowers:	up to 3mm.
Leaves:	**linear** to **lance shaped** to **oval**.

Knotgrass

Knotweed family

Flowering: Jul - Oct   Seeds: Aug - Sep

Northern Knotgrass

Shakespeare mentions "the hindering knotgrass" in *A Midsummer Night's Dream* (Shakespeare 2007), as it was believed it could retard the growth of children or animals.

Knotgrass

Ray's Knotgrass

Pipewort *Eriocaulon aquaticum*/Piobhan Uisge

Habitat: local but frequent in the shallow fringes of acidic lochs in the moorland NE of Arinagour, Coll.

The grey-white, domed 'button head' flowers grow on leafless, emergent stems. From a distance, they look like knitting needles protruding from the water. The tiny 'button head' is itself made up of a series of minute, closely packed flowers, each with two grey **sepals** and two paler grey petals. Each flower has a small, black **bract**. The leaves have flattened sides and are translucent.

Form: **erect**, 20cm-60cm, (can reach 150cm).

Flowers: **flower-head**, 5mm-12mm across with flowers 4mm long.

Leaves: **basal** tuft of **sword-shaped** leaves, 5cm-10cm long.

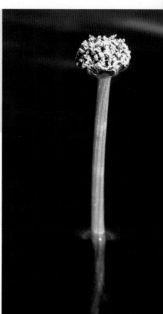

One of Coll's real specialities, this essentially North American species was first discovered on Coll in 1819 and has a very limited distribution in Ireland and parts of W Scotland. On Coll, it is confined to a compact area NE of Arinagour. For a distribution map, see *A Flora of Tiree, Gunna and Coll* (Pearman 2000).

Pipewort family

Flowering: Jul - Sep

Common Juniper *Juniperus communis subsp. nana*/Aiteann

Habitat: widespread, but local, on heath in the NE of Coll.

On Coll, Common Juniper of the form *nana* is found hugging the protruding rocks in the heather-dominated parts of the island. The stiff, needle-like, bluish-green leaves emerge from woody stems and the distinctive, berry-like cones are green in the first year and blue-black in the second. The flowers of the female plant are green and oval, while those on the male plant are yellow. The form *communis* is the more familiar shrubby bush of the Caledonian Forest and does not occur on the islands.

Form:	**prostrate**, up to 2m long.
Leaves:	**whorls** of 3, 4mm-12mm long, with a spiny tip.
Fruit:	berry-like cones.

The woody stems of Juniper were used in W Scotland for flavouring kippers. When burnt, it is almost smokeless and was used for fuelling illicit whisky stills. In traditional Pictish houses, the branches were used in conjunction with heather as insulation in cavity walls. Burning Juniper in the house was thought to ward off evil spirits and was used on Colonsay to fumigate houses harbouring infectious diseases and to prevent the Plague. On Barra, Juniper branches were used to replicate palms on Palm Sunday. Juniper berries provide a delicious flavouring for game dishes, and of course are the main flavouring in the production of gin.

Juniper family

Flowering: June

Round-leaved Sundew *Drosera rotundifolia*/Lus na Fèarnaich
Oblong-leaved Sundew *Drosera intermedia*/Dealt Ruaidhe
Great Sundew *Drosera anglica*/Lus a' Ghadmainn

Habitat: Sundews occur in very wet, very acidic conditions in bogs, and can be locally frequent.

Round-leaved Sundew

Form: **erect**, up to 10cm, (can reach 25cm).

Flowers: 5mm across.

Leaves: rounded, up to 1cm across.

Sundews are small **perennial** herbs with simple, long-stalked leaves in a **basal rosette**. All have very similar flowers with five to eight tiny, white petals, which only open briefly in sunshine. Oblong-leaved is the smallest, with stems that are barely longer than the stalked leaves. Like Round-leaved, its stem arises from below the leaf **rosette**. The flower of the Great Sundew can rise to twice the length of its stalked leaves and springs from the centre of its **rosette**. Aside from the variance in leaf shape and length of leaf stalk, these species can be distinguished by the lack of hairs on the Oblong-leaved leaf stalks, and the manner in which the hairy leaf stalks of the Round-leaved spread horizontally. The leaves are covered with sticky, red-tipped hairs that bear glue-producing glands. Small insects, usually midges, but sometimes damselflies, are trapped and then digested. It is thought that this supplements the plant's nitrate nutrition, as their bog habitats are relatively deficient in nutrients.

Sundew family

Flowering: Jun - Aug

Oblong-leaved Sundew

Form: **erect**, up to 5cm,
(can reach 10cm).

Flowers: 5mm across.

Leaves: oblong, with
blades up to 1cm.

Sundews have many uses. Finland still exports commercial quantities to Switzerland for medicines for respiratory disorders, and, commonly in the Hebrides, it was used for curdling milk to make butter and cheese. The sticky leaves, like those of the similarly insectivorous plants Pale and Common Butterwort (pages 77 & 41), have enzymes that can replace rennet.

Great Sundew

Form: **erect**, up to 20cm,
(can reach 30cm).

Flowers: 5mm across.

Leaves: oblong to **oval**, with
blades up to 4cm long.

Knotted Pearlwort *Sagina nodosa*/Mungan Snaimte
Procumbent Pearlwort *Sagina procumbens*/Mungan Làir

Habitat: Knotted Pearlwort is locally frequent in wet marshy places and bare, damp patches in grassland. Procumbent Pearlwort is very common on bare ground and in short grasslands.

Knotted Pearlwort

Form: **prostrate** or **erect**, 3cm-10cm.

Flowers: up to 1cm across.

Leaves: narrow, **linear**, pointed.

Knotted and Procumbent Pearlwort are inconspicuous, tufted, **perennial** plants of bare ground. Many of the similar pearlworts and spurreys are weedy species of disturbed habitats, while some, such as Knotted Pearlwort, occur as a natural component of wet machair. Procumbent Pearlwort has a central, non-flowering **rosette**, from which grow rooting runners that then turn up and bear the flowers. Its flowers have four green **sepals**, which dwarf the sometimes absent minute, greenish-white petals, while Knotted Pearlwort has five white, un-notched petals, twice the length of **sepals**. Knotted Pearlwort can also be distinguished by running your finger gently up the stem, thereby feeling the lateral clusters on the stem, which give the 'knotted' appearance. Pearlwort grows in wet, marshy places and is a charming sight in late summer.

Procumbent Pearlwort was once said to be the plant that Jesus first stepped on as he returned after the Resurrection.

Procumbent Pearlwort

Form: **prostrate** to **erect**, 1cm-3cm.

Flowers: 5mm across.

Leaves: **linear**.

  Knotted Pearlwort: Flowering: Jul - Sep

Procumbent Pearlwort: Flowering: May - Sep

Pink family

Brookweed *Samolus valerandi*/Luibh an t-Sruthain

Habitat: occasional in damp grassland, wet flushes, and by burns, particularly near the sea.

This unusual member of the primrose family is usually found close to the coast. Its **basal rosette** of leaves resembles that of the Daisy (page 138). The stem is hairless and the cup-shaped flowers have long stalks and five petals. The tiny white petals are joined near the base to form a **tube**. Brookweed can be confused with other small white flowers, particularly the cresses (e.g., Water-cress, page 148) and scurvygrasses (page 153) in the cabbage family, but the five petals (as opposed to four) are an identifying feature. The plant looks shiny and is slightly fleshy.

Form: **erect**, 5cm-45cm.

Flowers: 2mm-4mm across.

Leaves: **basal rosette** and **alternate** stem leaves, **spoon shaped**, 1cm-8cm long.

Druids protected their cattle from infectious diseases by placing Brookweed in their water troughs. It is now known that the edible, but bitter, leaves prevent scurvy - so the Druids were right to put it in their water troughs!

Primrose family

Fairy Flax *Linum catharticum*/Lìon nam Ban-sìdh

Habitat: widespread in sand dunes, machair and in base-rich grassland.

This pretty little herb can often be overlooked in the summer riot of colour. With slender (occasionally branched) stems, leaves that almost clasp the stem and tiny groups of five-petalled, white flowers, it is very similar to other small, delicate, white-flowered plants. Closer examination is needed to identify its distinguishing features: a hairless, upright, wiry stem; a yellow blotch at the base of its five narrow petals and unstalked, **opposite**, oblong leaves. Fairy Flax can also be identified by the way that its delicate flowers droop and only open in the sun; yet when it is in fruit, it stands erect.

Form: **erect**, 5cm-10cm, (can reach up to 25cm).

Flowers: 4mm-6mm across.

Leaves: **opposite**, oblong, very finely and evenly **toothed** like a saw, up to 1cm long.

Fruit: small, round **capsules**.

In Gaelic, Fairy Flax is also known as Miosach, which translates as 'monthly'. The plant was often used to treat menstrual problems. The Latin word *catharticum* translates as 'cathartic', and the plant is sometimes known as 'purging flax' as it can be used as a purgative and laxative.

Flax family

Flowering: Jun - Sep

Common Chickweed *Stellaria media*/Fliodh

Habitat: Common Chickweed is found on cultivated and open ground.

Common Chickweed is a common and widespread plant. It has a single line of hairs on its round, much-branched stem. The flower has five petals that are so deeply divided there appear to be ten, and its five long **sepals** form a green star on the outside of the petals. The lower leaves are long stalked, while the other leaves are unstalked. The very similar Bog Stitchwort, which only flowers in May and June, is found in wetter areas and prefers more acidic ground. It can be distinguished from Common Chickweed by its hairless, square stem, and more oval to lance-shaped leaves which are all unstalked. Although it too has five petals, these are shorter than the **sepals**, while for Common Chickweed the petals are the same length as the **sepals**.

Form:	**sprawling,** 5cm-40cm, (can reach 50cm).
Flowers:	5mm-10mm across.
Leaves:	**opposite** pairs, **heart shaped**, 5mm-30mm.

Common Chickweed is one of the world's most successful plants as it is able to flower in any month of the year. It can be abundant where the ground is enriched by cattle dung. It is a good source of vitamin C, and is still collected locally for salads. It has also been made into an ointment or poultice for skin complaints.

Pink family

Flowering: all year

167

Marsh Pennywort *Hydrocotyle vulgaris*/Lus na Peighinn

Habitat: locally common in wet grassland, by lochs, and around bogs.

Marsh Pennywort is often overlooked as it is a small, mat-forming plant that rarely bears flowers. The flowers are tiny and greenish-white in colour. They can sometimes be found underneath the leaves, which are held up like a parasol by the central stalk. Although the leaves are often overshadowed by taller plants, Marsh Pennywort can be abundant.

Form: **creeping**, forms mats up to 30cm.

Flowers: 1mm.

Leaves: **circular**, shallow **toothed**, 1cm-5cm wide.

Carrot family

   Flowering: Jun - Aug

Cleavers *Galium aparine*/Garbh-lus

Habitat: widespread and frequent on enriched and disturbed ground, on beaches, ditches, and grassland.

This well-known plant is immediately identified by the rough, square stem lined with backward-pointing prickles, which enable it to clamber up and over other plants or potential supports. The leaves also have backward-pointing prickles along the edges. The fruits are green, then purple when ripe, and are covered with tiny, hooked bristles. The small groups of tiny, white flowers are often overlooked.

Pliny (111-113AD) said "A pottage of cleavers, a little mutton and oatmeal is good to cause lankness and keep from fatness". The seeds can be roasted and used as coffee, while an infusion of leaves makes a soothing tea. Ointments for skin problems are still used today. The Gaelic name, 'rough plant', reflects the roughness .of the stem, while the alternate common English name of Sticky Willy reflects the plant's ability to stick to clothing.

Form: **prostrate** and scrambling to 100cm, (can reach 300cm).

Flowers: 2mm-3mm across.

Leaves: 6-8 in a **whorl**, **linear** to **lance shaped**, 12mm-50mm long.

Fruit: 4mm-6mm long, oval.

Bedstraw family

Common Marsh-bedstraw *Galium palustre subsp. palustre/*Màdar Lèana
Heath Bedstraw *Galium saxatile/*Màdar Fraoich

Habitat: Common Marsh-bedstraw is common in wet areas; Heath Bedstraw is common in heath and acidic grasslands.

Common Marsh-bedstraw

Form: **creeping to erect**, up to 80cm, (can reach 100cm).

Flowers: 3mm across.

Leaves: **whorls**, oblong to **lance shaped**, backward pointing prickles on leaf edges, up to 3cm long.

These two bedstraws have square, hairless stems, with regularly spaced **whorls** of leaves. The small, white flowers are carried in clusters at the end of the flower-stalk. Common Marsh-bedstraw is taller and occurs in marshy, damp habitats. Heath Bedstraw is shorter and compact, and is found in heathy or acidic habitats. Check whether the prickles on the leaf edges point backwards or forwards.

The latin name *Galium* comes from the Greek word 'Gala', meaning milk. Bedstraws were once widely used in curdling milk to make cheese.

Heath Bedstraw

Form: mat forming/**erect**, up to 10cm, (can reach 30cm).

Flowers: 3mm across.

Leaves: **whorls**, oval to **lance shaped**, forward pointing prickles on leaf edges, up to 1cm long.

Bedstraw family

 Marsh

  Heath

Flowering: May - Aug

Local stories

From Coll:

Catriona Young's family moved to Coll in the early 1970s. Catriona spent some years off the island for her secondary and university education, but returned to live on Coll in 1998, with her husband Doug (who has helped with Gaelic translations for this book). They live in the West End of Coll with their three girls, Berryblack the horse, and a dog called Dave. Aside from working part time, Catriona is very active in a number of community projects.

Coll Herbals

Coll Herbals began in 1974, on a very small scale, from the family home of Wendy Mckechnie. It then spread into two caravans at the back of the house and eventually, in 1978, into a much larger factory at the old schoolhouse in Arinagour village.

Local flowers were often used and were infused into scented oils; wild Rose and honeysuckle were the main scented oils, and also 'Ceol-na-mara', which was a blend of rosemary, myrtle, honeysuckle and heather, all locally picked and infused with mineral oil to form the perfume oils.

There were three main creams that used local flowers: rose hand cream; honeysuckle night cream and home grown marigold night cream. Shampoo was made from chamomile, there was a rosemary hair brightener, and, latterly, myrtle was used in oil as an insect repellent.

My mother, Wendy Mckechnie, experimented with extracts of many local flowers, but not all went into production; examples are: Thyme oil (which was a wonderful deep violet colour); Rowan; Willow Bark; Rosehips; Eyebright, and she also made

Rowan berries

Orris root powder from dried and powdered Iris bulbs (which was used as a preservative).

As the business expanded, it became necessary to buy all the essential oils from off the island. Ironically, they were bought from Switzerland, as it was the only supplier Mum could buy from in small quantities.

Another stage of Herbals' development was the production of dried herbs and flowers, which were used for making scented sachets, pillows and duvets (which, in the late 70s, sold for a staggering £2, £25, and £90, respectively). They were filled with dried and scented local flowers and herbs such as myrtle, honeysuckle, rose, and lavender. Many a local teenager was employed to pick the petals and myrtle, and it was a very sociable and jolly summer activity, which I often participated in as a child.

Catriona Young

From Tiree:

*Thrift has many names: in English it is also known as Sea Pink; and there are two Gaelic names recorded in this book (see page 69). Here is a story from An Iodhlann (Tiree's historical centre www. aniodhlann.org.uk) about the local Gaelic name, **barr a' chinn**.*

Barr a' chinn (top of the head) was a common disease affecting children on Tiree, although not found elsewhere, and was usually caused by a fright. The child would become pale, listless and lose his or her appetite. It was said the condition was caused by the descent of two bones in the roof of the mouth.

There were two cures, physical and herbal. In the physical cure, the healer's index and middle finger or thumb was pressed against the roof of the mouth, pushing the 'bones' back. This is remembered as being quite painful.

The herbal treatment used the plant Sea Pink, known locally as **barr a' chinn**. This was collected on the day of the treatment, dried

Barr a' chinn

by the fire then put into a small cotton or linen bag which was sewn onto the patient's vest. Both treatments were accompanied by a rhyme.

An Iodhlann

From Coll:

B and Kenneth Cassels have been coming to Coll every year for almost 60 years. In that time they have seen many changes on the island. The extension to their house was built from stone procured from the blasting of the road down to the New Pier. The Craigdarroch garden is B and Kenneth's pride and joy. In recent years it has been used as a focal point for nature trips from the Nursery, as there is such a wealth of plant life to be seen.

Years of interest

Our first 'Flora for Coll' was an old, red exercise book, which we compiled when we came to the island about 1950, augmented by many visits since. We have always been interested in the natural world – the birds, beasts and flowers – and we were soon making lists of what we saw, spurred on by our children's questions.

In those days there were only three cars on the island; roads were largely unfenced and stocking was much lighter. Increased grazing has contributed to the disappearance of a number of plants, and some only survive in gardens that have been fenced for many years (e.g. Woundwort in the Craigdarroch garden).

In the 1980s, we got to know Joan Clark, who was the official Flower Recorder for the island. She checked our original records and guided us towards a more scientific approach. This amended record has contributed to the production of this book, but the old red book has been consulted too!

Joan was a brilliant and dedicated botanist. Even

Marsh Woundwort

in her late eighties, and having had two hip replacements, she
tramped all over the island with inexhaustible enthusiasm and
taught us so much.

In the seventies, when the children's classes for the Coll Show
included 'a bunch of wild flowers' we were horrified to see a
stack of Irish Lady's-tresses. To make matters worse the child
could not remember where she had picked it!

B and Kenneth Cassels

From Coll:

*Archie Sproat was born and brought up on Coll. His interest in
the natural world leans more to the sea than the land and he is
often seen out in his boat, which he moors at Arinagour Old Pier.
You can read his story of lobster fishing in the Coll Magazine
(issue 20). Here is his tale of his first taste of sorrel leaves.*

Around about 1950/51, when I was about 10 years old, a couple

Common Sorrel

of children from Ayrshire came
to spend a few weeks of their
summer holidays with relatives
in Coll. They told us about this
plant, that you could chew,
which they called soorag
(sorrel) We were a bit doubtful,
as we had all been told that,
if you chewed dandelions, it
made you wet the bed, so we
wondered what soorag would
make you do! However, we
decided to try it out. I was not
too impressed with the taste
and, to be honest, did not ever
bother to chew it again after
our two playmates returned to
the mainland.

Archie Sproat

Illustrated glossary

Flower anatomy

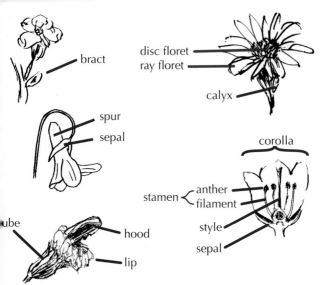

bract

disc floret
ray floret

calyx

spur
sepal

corolla

stamen — anther
filament

style

sepal

tube

hood

lip

Early-purple Orchid

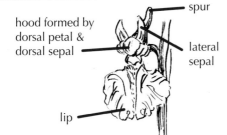

spur

hood formed by
dorsal petal &
dorsal sepal

lateral
sepal

lip

Fruit

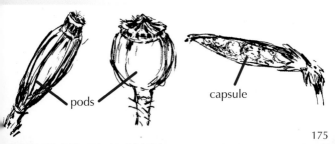

pods

capsule

Leaf shapes and examples

arrow shaped
Autumn Hawkbit

circular
Marsh Pennywort

heart shaped
Grass-of-Parnassus

kidney shaped
Marsh-marigold

lance shaped
Ribwort Plantain

linear
Harebell

oval
Red Clover

spear shaped
Common Sorrel

spoon shaped
Daisy

sword shaped
Ragged-Robin

tear-drop shaped
Water Mint

mid-rib
Red Clover

tendril

opposite leaflets
Bush Vetch

alternate leaflets
Silverweed

palmate
Bloody Crane's-bill

single pinnate
Sea Rocket

2-3 times pinnate
Sea Mayweed

toothed
Water Mint

broadly toothed
Cat's-ear

tri-foliate
White Clover

whorl

whorl
Common Marsh-bedstraw

Glossary

Listed below are all the words that you will see highlighted in bold throughout the flower accounts.

Alternate: where the stem leaves (or leaflets) occur first on one side and then the other, see p177.

Anther: the sac which contains the pollen (part of the **stamen**) p175.

Arrow shaped: see p176.

Auricle: an earlike lobe or pair of lobes which clasp the stem at the base of a leaf.

Basal: at the bottom or base (**basal rosette**).

Bract: a leaf with a flower in the angle between the leaf and plant stem, see p175.

Calyx: refers collectively to the group of **sepals** at the base of a flower-head, see p175.

Calcareous: soil that is rich in calcium, which on the islands comes from the remains of sea shells blown ashore as sand.

Capsule: a dry fruit that opens to release the seeds, see p175.

Circular: see p176.

Climbing: use of vegetation or other matter to reach upwards.

Corolla: refers collectively to the petals of a flower, see p175.

Creeping: generally refers to plants whose stems run along the ground and then rise up to bear the flower (written as creeping to erect); it can also mean mat forming.

Disc florets: tubular small flowers in the centre of a **flower-head** see p175.

Dorsal petal: the petal at the back of an orchid, see p175.

Dorsal sepal: the **sepal** at the back of an orchid, see p175.

Erect: refers to a plant that holds itself upright.

Flower-head: a close **inflorescence** where individual flowers all grow together at the tip of the stem.

Floret: a small flower, see p175.

Glaucous: sea green or greyish blue.

Heart shaped: see p176.

Hood: the upper lobe(s) of the **corolla**, see p175.

Inflorescence: the arrangement of flowers on a plant.

Kidney shaped: see p176.

Lance shaped: see p176.

Lateral sepal: the **sepal** found on the side(s) of an orchid, see p175.

Linear: see p176.

Lip: the lower lobe of the **corolla** (or occasionally the **calyx**), see p175.

Mid-rib: the main vein of the leaf running along its centre, see p177.

Opposite: where the leaves (or leaflets) appear in pairs on either side of the stem or stalk, see p177.

Oval: see p176.

Palmate: a compound leaf which is comprised of more than three leaflets which appear at the end of the leaf stalk, see p177.

Perennial: a plant that lives for more than two years.

Pinnate: a compound leaf which is comprised of individual leaflets (usually in **opposite** pairs) which appear along the leaf stalk; often with a terminal leaflet, see p177.

Pods: the fruit or its shell, see p175.

Pollinia: a mass of pollen grains which have stuck together (pollinium: singular).

Prostrate: refers to plants that lie on the ground.

Raceme: an **inflorescence** consisting of stalked flowers on the stem, which bloom from the bottom up.

Ray florets: tubular small flowers that spread outwards, see p175.

Rhizomes: a creeping underground stem.

Rosette: a circle of leaves.

Sepal: refers to an individual floral leaf (usually green) which surrounds the petals at their base, see p175.

Spear shaped: see p176.

Spike: an **inflorescence** where stalkless flowers are arranged on the axis of the stem.

Spoon shaped: see p176.

Sprawling: plants that climb in any old fashion, upwards or outwards.

Spur: usually contains nectar, and is the projection from around the base or back of the petals or **sepals**, see p175.

Stamen: the individual male organ of the flower, it consists of the filament and the **anther**, see p175.

Stipules: (usually) a pair of leaf-like appendages appearing at the base of the leaf stalk.

Style: the stalk-like structure which bears the pollen and emanates from the flower's ovaries, see p175.

Sword shaped: see p176.

Tear-drop shaped: see p176.

Tendrils: a shoot emerging from the leaf or main stem which the plant uses to climb other vegetation (or other nearby item such as a fence), see p177.

Toothed: implies that the leaf does not have a smooth edge. The degree to which a leaf is toothed varies enormously, see p177.

Trailing refers to plants that either lie on the ground or on surrounding vegetation. The stem is not sufficiently robust to hold erect.

Trifoliate: a compound leaf which is comprised of three leaflets only, see p177.

Tube: formed by fused sepals or petals, see p175.

Umbel: a flat-topped **inflorescence**.

Umbellifer: generally, a plant with **umbels**.

Untoothed: with a smooth edge.

Whorl: a number of flowers or leaves appearing at the same point. See p177.

Respect our islands

Coll and Tiree are spectacular in their unspoilt beauty. Access rights come with responsibility. Please use your common sense and keep to these guidelines:

- Respect islanders' right to privacy by keeping a reasonable distance from private houses and gardens.
- Respect islanders' rights to work safely and effectively by keeping a safe distance, particularly if there are dangerous activities being carried out.
- Leave gates as you find them.
- Do not block or obstruct an entrance or track.
- Do not feed animals.
- Use local advice so that you can take account of shooting.
- Do not damage fences or walls.
- Avoid damage to crops by using paths and tracks, by using the margins of the field, or by going over ground that hasn't been planted.
- Take your litter home.
- Treat places with care: leave them as you find them.
- Keep your dog under proper control. Do not take dogs into fields where there are young animals present. If you go into a field of farm animals, keep your dog on a short lead or under close control and keep as far as possible from the animals.

For more information, please visit www.outdooraccess-scotland.com

Publications and websites about Tiree and Coll

An Tirisdeach, Tiree's fortnightly newsletter. Email: antirisdeach@tireebroadband.com, or write to The Island Centre, Crossapol, Isle of Tiree, Argyll, PA77 6UP.

Or visit: www.isleoftiree.com

Coll Magazine, Coll's annual magazine. Visit www.collmagazine.co.uk or write to The Editor, Kilbride, Isle of Coll, Argyll, PA78 6TB.

Or visit: www.visitcoll.co.uk

Bowler, John and Hunter, Janet. *Birds of Tiree and Coll*. Paircwood Publishing, 2007.

Please do not pick the plants.
Leave for others to enjoy!

For further information on wildflowers and the law, please see www.bsbi.org.uk or www.snh.org.uk

---

Recommended reading

In addition to those listed in the bibliography, many of the following have been used as reference in compiling this book.

Allan, Brian and Woods, Patrick. *Wild Orchids of Scotland*. HMSO, 1993.

Cheffings, Christine and Farrell, Lynne. *The Vascular Plant Red Data List for Great Britain*. Joint Nature Conservative Committee, Peterborough, 2005.

Clark, Joan and MacDonald, Ian. *Ainmean Gaidhlig Lusan–Gaelic Names of Plants*. Private publisher, 1999.

Clapham, Arthur and Tutin, Thomas and Warburg, Edmund. *Excursion Flora of the British Isles*. Cambridge University Press, 1981.

Dony, John and Jury, Stephen and Perring, Franklyn. *English Names of Wild Flowers*. BSBI, 1986.

Fitter, Richard and Fitter, Alistair and Farrer, Ann. *Pocket Guide to Grasses, Sedges, Rushes and Ferns*. Collins, 1984.

Fletcher, Neil. *Wild Flowers*. Dorling Kindersley, 2004.

Fletcher, Neil and Tomblin, Gill. *The Easy Wildflower Guide*. Aurum Press Ltd 2005.

Lang, David. *Britain's Orchids*. WILD guides, 2004.

Rose, Francis. *The Wild Flower Key*. Penguin Books Ltd, 1991.

Scott, Michael. *Scottish Wild Flowers*. Collins, 2000.

Stace, Clive. *New Flora of the British Isles*. Cambridge Universtiy Press, 1997.

Sutton, David. *Field Guide to the Wild Flowers of Britain and Northern Europe*. Larousse, 1996.

Wren, Richard. *Potter's New Cyclopaedia of Botanical Drugs and Preparations*. Health Science Press, 1988.

Bibliography

Clyne, Douglas. *Gaelic Names of Flowers and Plants*. Crùisgean, 1989.
Grieve, Maude, F.R.H.S. *A Modern Herbal*. Dover Publications, 1931.
Gunn, Neil. *Off in a Boat*. House of Lochar, 2000.
Jumbalaya, Johnny. *Really Wild Food Guide*. Jumbalaya, 2002.
Milliken, William and Bridgewater, Sam. *Flora Celtica*. Birlinn, 2004.
Orczy, Baroness. *The Scarlet Pimpernel*. Hodder & Stoughton Paperbacks, 2005.
Pearman, David and Preston, Chris. *A Flora of Tiree, Gunna & Coll*. Dorchester, 2000.
Shakespeare, William. *A Midsummer Night's Dream*. Penguin Popular Classics, 2007.

Index of common names

To make it easy for the reader to find plants, many have two listings, e.g., Water Mint can be found under Water and under Mint. Listings in parenthesis do not have a full account, but are mentioned in another plant's account.

Amphibious Bistort, 62
Angelica, Wild, 129
Asphodel, Bog, 112
Autumn Hawkbit, 95
Babington's Orache, 124
Bartsia, Red, 74
Bedstraw, Common Marsh-, 170
    Heath, 170
    Lady's, 98
Bell Heather, 44
Bindweed, Large, 137
    Sea, 53
Bird's-foot-trefoil, Common, 109
    Greater, 109
Bistort, Amphibious, 62
Biting Stonecrop, 113
Bloody Crane's-bill, 64
Bluebell, 32
Blue Water-speedwell, 42
Bog Asphodel, 112
Bogbean, 141
Bog-myrtle, 116
Bog Pimpernel, 78
(Bog Stitchwort), 156, 167
Bramble, 143
Branched Bur-reed, 122
Brookweed, 165
(Buck's-horn Plantain), 114
Bugloss, 49
Bulbous Buttercup, 104
Burdock, Wood, 60
Burnet Rose, 142
Bur-reed, Branched, 122
Bush Vetch, 39
Butterbur, 61
Buttercup, Bulbous, 104
    Creeping, 104
    Meadow, 104
Butterfly-orchid, (Greater), 135
    Lesser, 135
Butterwort, Common, 41
    Pale, 77
Campion, Red, 66
    Sea, 144
Carrot, Wild, 133
    (Sea), 133
Cat's-ear, 95
Celandine, Lesser, 102
Centaury, Common, 76
(Chamomile), 139
Chickweed, Common, 167
Cinquefoil, Marsh, 67
Cleavers, 169
Clover, Red, 68
    White, 146
Colt's-foot, 90
Common Bird's-foot-trefoil, 109

Common Butterwort, 41
Common Centaury, 76
Common Chickweed, 167
Common Cottongrass, 140
(Common Cow-wheat), p100
Common Dog-violet, 40
(Common Hemp-nettle), 20, 27
Common Juniper, 161
Common Knapweed, 25
Common Marsh-bedstraw, 170
Common Milkwort, 46
Common Mouse-ear, 156
(Common Poppy), 52
Common Ragwort, 91
Common Reed, 21
Common Sorrel, 80
Common Scurvygrass, 153
Common Spotted-orchid, 55
Common Stork's-bill, 75
Common Twayblade, 123
Corn Marigold, 92
Cottongrass, Common, 140
    Hare's-tail, 140
Cow Parsley, 132
(Cow-wheat, Common), 100
Crane's-bill, Bloody, 64
    Dove's-foot, 75
Creeping Buttercup, 104
Creeping Thistle, 24
Cross-leaved Heath, 44
Cuckooflower, 71
Curled Dock, 80
(Cut-leaved Dead-nettle), 73
Daisy, 138
    Oxeye, 138
Dandelion, 94
Danish Scurvygrass, 153
Dead-nettle, (Cut-leaved), 73
    (Northern), 73
    Red, 73
Devil's-bit Scabious, 34
Dock, Curled, 80
(Dog Rose), 142
Dog-violet, Common, 40
    (Heath), 40
Dove's-foot Crane's-bill, 75
Early Marsh-orchid, 56
Early-purple Orchid, 28
Elecampane, 87
English Stonecrop, 152
(Equal-leaved Knotgrass), 158
Everlasting, Mountain, 150
Eyebright, 154 - 155
Fairy Flax, 166
Fat-hen, 126
Field Gentian, 38
Field Forget-me-not, 50
Flax, Fairy, 166

Forget-me-not, Field, 50
    Tufted, 50,
    (Water), 50
Fragrant-orchid, Heath, 57
    (Marsh) 57,
Frog Orchid, 125
Gentian, Field, 38
Germander Speedwell, 42
Gorse, 108
Grass-of-Parnassus, 145
Great Sundew, 162
Great Willowherb, 54
(Greater Butterfly-orchid), 135
Greater Bird's-foot-trefoil, 109
(Greater Plantain), 114
(Greater Spearwort), 103
Groundsel, 119
Harebell, 31
Hare's-tail Cottongrass, 140
Hawkbit, Autumn, 95
Hawk's-beard, Smooth, 94
(Hawkweed, Mouse-ear), 95
Heath Bedstraw, 170
Heath, Cross-leaved, 44
(Heath Dog-violet), 40
Heath Fragrant-orchid, 57
(Heath Milkwort), 46
Heath Spotted-orchid, 58
Heather, 44
    Bell, 44
(Hedge Woundwort), 27
(Hemlock Water-dropwort), 130
(Hemp-nettle, Common), 20, 27
Hoary Willowherb, 72
Hogweed, 129
holly, Sea-, 22
Honeysuckle, 86
Iris, Yellow, 85
Irish Lady's-tresses, 136
Juniper, Common, 161
Kidney Vetch, 93
Knapweed, Common, 25
Knotgrass, 158
    (Equal-leaved), 158
    (Northern), 158
    (Ray's), 158
Knotted Pearlwort, 164
Lady's Bedstraw, 98
Lady's-tresses, Irish, 136
Large Bindweed, 137
Lesser Butterfly-orchid, 135
Lesser Celandine, 102
Lesser Meadow-rue, 117
Lesser Spearwort, 103
Lesser Water-plantain, 149
Lobelia, Water, 47
Long-headed Poppy, 52
loosestrife, Purple-, 20
Lousewort, 70
    Marsh, 70
Marigold, Corn, 92
    Marsh-, 102
Marram, 121
Marsh-bedstraw, Common, 170

Marsh Cinquefoil, 66
(Marsh Fragrant-orchid), 57
Marsh Lousewort, 70
Marsh-orchid, Early, 56
    Northern, 29
Marsh Pennywort, 168
Marsh Ragwort, 91
Marsh Speedwell, 42
Marsh St. John's-wort, 111
Marsh Thistle, 24
Marsh Willowherb, 72
Marsh Woundwort, 27
Marsh-marigold, 102
Mayweed, (Scentless), 139
    Sea, 139
Meadow Buttercup, 104
Meadow-rue, Lesser, 117
Meadowsweet, 131
Meadow Vetchling, 110
Milk-vetch, Purple, 30
Milkwort, Common, 46
    (Heath), 46
    Sea-, 81
Mint, Water, 35
Montbretia, 82
Mountain Everlasting, 150
Mouse-ear, Common, 156
    (Sea), 156
    (Sticky), 156
(Mouse-ear Hawkweed), 95
Mugwort, 84
myrtle, Bog-, 116
(Northern Dead-nettle), 73
(Northern Knotgrass), 158
Northern Marsh-orchid, 29
Oblong-leaved Sundew, 162
Orache Babington's, 124
Orchid, Common Spotted-, 55
    Common Twayblade, 123
    Early Marsh-, 56
    Early-purple, 28
    Frog, 125
    (Greater Butterfly-), 135
    Heath Fragrant-, 57
    Heath Spotted-, 58
    Irish Lady's-tresses, 136
    Lesser Butterfly-, 135
    (Marsh Fragrant-), 57
    Northern Marsh-, 29
    Pyramidal, 59
Oxeye Daisy, 138
Oysterplant, 36
Pale Butterwort, 77
Pansy, Wild, 26
Parsley, Cow, 132
Parsley Water-dropwort, 130
Pearlwort, Knotted, 164
    Procumbent, 164
Pennywort, Marsh, 168
Perennial Sow-thistle, 88
(Pignut), 133
Pimpernel, Bog, 78
    Scarlet, 79
Pineappleweed, 101

Pipewort, 160
Plantain, (Buck's-horn), 114
      (Greater), 114
      Lesser Water-, 149
      Ribwort, 114
      (Sea), 114
(Poppy, Common), 52
      Long-headed, 52
Prickly Sow-thistle, 88
Primrose, 96
Procumbent Pearlwort, 164
Purple-loosestrife, 20
Purple Milk-vetch, 30
Pyramidal Orchid, 59
Ragged-Robin, 65
Ragwort, Common, 91
      Marsh, 91
(Ray's Knotgrass), 158
Red Bartsia, 74
Red Clover, 68
Red Campion, 66
Red Dead-nettle, 73
Redshank, 63
Reed, Common, 21
Ribwort Plantain, 114
Rock-rose, Spotted, 99
Rocket, Sea, 147
Rosebay Willowherb, 54
Rose, Burnet, 142
      (Dog), 142
      Spotted rock-, 99
Roseroot, 97
Round-leaved Sundew, 162
St. John's-wort, Marsh, 111
      Slender, 107
      Square-stalked, 107
Sandwort, Sea, 157
Scabious, Devil's-bit, 34
Scarlet Pimpernel, 79
(Scentless Mayweed), 139
Scurvygrass, Common, 153
      Danish, 153
Sea Bindweed, 53
Sea Campion, 144
(Sea Carrot), 133
Sea Mayweed, 139
(Sea Mouse-ear), 156
(Sea Plantain), 114
Sea Rocket, 147
Sea Sandwort, 157
Sea-holly, 22
Sea-milkwort, 81
Selfheal, 37
Sheep's Sorrel, 80
Shepherd's-purse, 151
Silverweed, 106
Slender St. John's-wort, 107
Smooth Hawk's-beard, 94
Smooth Sow-thistle, 88
Sneezewort, 134
Sorrel, Common, 80
      Sheep's, 80
Sow-thistle, Perennial, 88
      Prickly, 88
      Smooth, 88

Spear Thistle, 23
Spearwort, (Greater), 103
      Lesser, 103
Speedwell, Blue Water-, 42
      Germander, 42
      Marsh, 42
      Wall, 42
Spring Squill, 33
Spotted-orchid, Common, 55
      Heath, 58
Spotted Rock-rose, 99
Square-stalked St. John's-wort, 107
Squill, Spring, 33
(Sticky Mouse-ear), 156
(Stitchwort, Bog), 156, 167
Stonecrop, Biting, 113
      English, 152
Stork's-bill, Common, 75
Sundew, Great, 162
      Oblong-leaved, 162
      Round-leaved, 162
Tansy, 101
Thistle, Creeping, 24
      Marsh, 24
      Spear, 23
Thread-leaved Water-crowfoot, 149
Thrift, 69
Thyme, Wild, 48
Tormentil, 118
Tufted Forget-me-not, 50
Tufted Vetch, 39
Twayblade, Common, 123
Vetch, Bush, 39
      Kidney, 93
      Purple milk-, 30
      Tufted, 39
Vetchling, Meadow, 110
Wall Speedwell, 42
Water-cress, 148
Water-crowfoot, Thread-leaved, 149
Water-dropwort, (Hemlock), 130
      Parsley, 130
(Water Forget-me-not), 50
Water-lily, White, 128
Water Lobelia, 47
Water Mint, 35
Water-plantain, Lesser, 149
Water-speedwell, Blue, 42
White Clover, 146
White Water-lily, 128
Wild Angelica, 129
Wild Carrot, 133
Wild Pansy, 26
Wild Thyme, 48
Willowherb, Great, 54
      Hoary, 72
      Marsh, 72
      Rosebay, 54
Wood Burdock, 60
Woundwort, (Hedge), 27
      Marsh, 27
Yarrow, 134
Yellow Iris, 85
Yellow-rattle, 100

Index of Latin names

Listings in parenthesis do not have a full account, but are mentioned in another plant's account.

Achillea millefolium, 134
    ptarmica, 134
Ammophila arenaria, 121
Anacamptis pyramidalis, 59
Anagallis arvensis subsp. arvensis, 79
    tenella, 78
Anchusa arvensis, 49
Angelica sylvestris, 129
Antennaria dioica, 150
Anthriscus sylvestris, 132
Anthyllis vulneraria, 93
Arctium nemorosum, 60
Armeria maritima, 69
Artemisia vulgaris, 84
Astragalus danicus, 30
Atriplex glabriuscula, 124
Baldellia ranunculoides, 149
Bellis perennis, 138
Cakile maritima, 147
Calluna vulgaris, 44
Caltha palustris, 102
Calystegia silvatica, 137
    soldanella, 53
Campanula rotundifolia, 31
Capsella bursa-pastoris, 151
Cardamine pratensis, 71
Centaurea nigra, 25
Centaurium erythraea, 76
Cerastium (diffusum), 156
    fontanum, 156
    (glomeratum) , 156
(Chamaemelum nobile), 139
Chamerion angustifolium, 54
Chenopodium album, 126
Chrysanthemum segetum, 92
Cirsium arvense, 24
    palustre, 24
    vulgare, 23
Cochlearia danica, 153
    officinalis, 153
(Conopodium majus), 133
Crepis capillaris, 94
Crocosmia, 82
Dactylorhiza fuchsia, 55
    incarnata, 56
    incarnata coccinea, 56
    maculata subsp. ericetorum, 58
    purpurella, 29
    viridis, 125
Daucus carota subsp. carota, 133
    subsp. gummifer, 133
Drosera anglica, 162
    intermedia, 162
    rotundifolia, 162

Epilobium hirsutum, 54
    palustre, 72
    parviflorum, 72
Erica cinerea, 44
    tetralix, 44
Eriocaulon aquaticum, 160
Eriophorum angustifolium, 140
    vaginatum, 140
Erodium cicutarium, 95
Eryngium maritimum, 22
Euphrasia heslop-harrisonii, 155
    nemorosa, 154
Filipendula ulmaria, 131
(Galeopsis tetrahit), 20, 27
Galium aparine, 169
    palustre subsp. palustre, 170
    saxatile, 170
    verum, 98
Gentianella campestris, 38
Geranium molle, 75
    sanguineum, 64
Glaux maritima, 81
Gymnadenia borealis, 57
    (densiflora), 57
Heracleum sphondylium, 129
Honckenya peploides, 157
Hyacinthoides non-scripta, 32
Hydrocotyle vulgaris, 168
Hypericum elodes, 111
    pulchrum, 107
    tetrapterum, 107
Hypochaeris radicata, 95
Inula helenium, 87
Iris pseudacorus, 85
Juniperus communis subsp nana, 161
Lamium (confertum), 73
    (hybridum), 73
    purpureum, 73
Lathyrus pratensis, 110
Leontodon autumnalis, 95
Leucanthemum vulgare, 138
Linum catharticum, 166
Listera ovata, 123
Lobelia dortmanna, 47
Lonicera periclymenum, 86
Lotus corniculatus, 109
    pedunculatus, 109
Lychnis flos-cuculi, 65
Lythrum salicaria, 20
Matricaria discoidea, 101
(Melampyrum pratense), 100
Mentha aquatica, 35
Menyanthes trifoliata, 141
Mertensia maritima, 36

Myosotis arvensis, 50
    laxa, 50
    (scorpoides), 50
Myrica gale, 116
Narthecium ossifragum, 112
Nymphaea alba, 128
Odontites vernus, 74
Oenanthe (crocata), 130
    lachenalii, 130
Orchis mascula, 28
Papaver dubium subsp. *dubium*, 52
    (rhoes) 52
Parnassia palustris, 145
Pedicularis palustris, 70
    sylvatica, 70
Persicaria amphibia, 62
    maculosa, 63
Petasites hybridus, 61
Phragmites australis, 21
(Pilosella officinarum)
Pinguicula lusitanica, 77
    vulgaris, 41
Plantago (coronopus), 114
    lanceolata, 114
    (major), 114
    (maritima), 114
Platanthera bifolia, 135
    (chlorantha), 135
Polygala (serpyllifolia), 46
    vulgaris, 46
Polygonum (arenastrum), 158
    aviculare, 158
    (boreale), 158
    (oxyspermum), 158
Potentilla anserina, 106
    erecta, 118
    palustris, 67
Primula vulgaris, 96
Prunella vulgaris, 37
Ranunculus acris, 104
    bulbosus, 104
    ficaria, 102
    flammula, 103
    (lingua), 103
    repens, 104
    trichophyllus, 149
Rhinanthus minor, 100
Rorippa nasturtium-aquaticum, 148

Rosa (canina), 142
    pimpinellifolia, 142
Rubus fruticosus , 143
Rumex acetosa, 80
    acetosella, 80
    crispus, 80
Sagina nodosa, 164
    procumbens, 164
Samolus valerandi, 165
Scilla verna, 33
Sedum acre, 113
    anglicum, 152
    rosea, 97
Senecio aquaticus, 91
    jacobaea, 91
    vulgaris, 119
Silene dioica, 66
    uniflora, 144
Sonchus arvensis, 88
    asper, 88
    oleraceus, 88
Spargamium erectum, 122
Spiranthes romanzoffiana , 136
Stachys palustris, 27
    (sylvatica), 27
Stellaria media, 167
    (uliginosa), 156, 167
Succisa pratensis, 34
Tanacetum vulgare, 101
Taraxacum officinale agg., 94
Thalictrum minus, 117
Thymus polytrichus, 48
Trifolium pratense, 68
    repens, 146
Tripleurospermum maritimum, 139
    (inodorum), 139
Tuberaria guttata subsp. *breweri*, 99
Tussilago farfara, 90
Ulex europaeus, 108
Veronica anagallis-aquatica, 42
    arvensis, 42
    chamaedrys, 42
    scutellata, 42
Vicia cracca, 39
    sepium, 39
Viola (canina), 40
    riviniana, 40
    tricolor subsp. *curtisii*, 26

About the project

Wild Flowers of Coll and Tiree has been a collaborative project between our two islands. Location of meetings depended on ferry timetables, the weather and childcare arrangements. On one occasion we hired the services of Skipinnish Sea Tours to facilitate the Tiree contingent arriving and departing on the same day; on another, we had a 'between ferry boats' meeting, with the Coll contingent travelling to Tiree on a Thursday. At other times, our meetings continued into the wee small hours, as we took advantage of local hospitality and stayed overnight.

Our intention has been to produce a book that is simple to use for those with no botanical knowledge, but also contains enough information to hold the interest of the more experienced botanist. The book also represents a snapshot of common flowers growing on Coll and Tiree. Decisions as to what to include and what to omit were very difficult. If you, the reader, feel that there has been a gross admission, we would be happy to hear from you and would consider additional mentions in future reprints. While each flower with an account has been photographed on either Tiree or Coll, there are a couple of instances where we have used shots from the SNH library to ensure a good quality image.

This book is unique in its combination of botanical information, photographic content and interesting facts and stories. We hope that it helps you to see the many levels of beauty on these two very special islands.

On a personal note, I would like to thank my husband, Pete, for his support and my children, Aidan, Ishbel and Caitlin, for their patience during the many hours I have spent glued to the computer.

Emma Grant

Author credits

John Bowler:

Autumn Hawkbit, Babington's Orache, Bluebell, Bush Vetch, Butterbur, Cat's–ear, Common Sorrel, Cuckooflower, Curled Dock, Dandelion, Elecampane, Grass-of-Parnassus, Great Willowherb, Hoary Willowherb, Honeysuckle, Kidney Vetch, Large Bindweed, Marsh Willowherb, Marsh Woundwort, Meadow Vetchling, Montbretia, Mugwort, Oysterplant, Perennial Sow-thistle, Prickly Sow-thistle, Purple-loosestrife, Purple Milk-vetch, Ragged-Robin, Red Campion, Rosebay Willowherb, Sea Bindweed, Sea Campion, Sea Sandwort, Sea-holly, Sheep's Sorrel, Smooth Hawk's-beard, Smooth Sow-thistle, Sneezewort, Spring Squilll, Tormentil, Tufted Vetch, Water Mint, Wood Burdock, Yarrow, Yellow Iris.

Emma Grant:

About the project, back page, Common Bird's-foot-trefoil, Common Centaury, four easy steps to flower identification, glossary, Greater Bird's-foot-trefoil, How to use this book, introductory colour sections, Red Clover.

Charlie Self:

Biting Stonecrop, Bog Asphodel, Bogbean, Bog-myrtle, Bog Pimpernel, Bramble, Branched Bur-reed, Brookweed, Bugloss, Bulbous Buttercup, Cleavers, Colt's-foot, Common Butterwort, Common Chickweed, Common Cottongrass, Common Marsh-bedstraw, Common Milkwort, Common Mouse-ear, Common Reed, Common Scurvygrass, Corn Marigold, Creeping Buttercup, Creeping Thistle, Daisy, Danish Scurvygrass, Devil's-bit Scabious, English Stonecrop, Eyebright, Fairy Flax, Fat-hen, Field Gentian, Field Forget-me-not, Germander Speedwell, Gorse, Great Sundew, Hare's-tail Cottongrass, Heath Bedstraw, Knotgrass, Knotted Pearlwort, Lady's Bedstraw, Lesser Celandine, Lesser Meadow-rue, Lesser Spearwort, Lousewort, Marram, Marsh Cinquefoil, Marsh Lousewort, Marsh-marigold, Marsh Pennywort, Marsh Speedwell, Marsh St. John's-wort, Marsh Thistle, Meadow Buttercup, Meadowsweet, Mountain Everlasting, Oblong-leaved Sundew, Oxeye Daisy, Pale Butterwort, Parsley Water-dropwort, Primrose, Procumbent Pearlwort, Ribwort Plantain, Round-leaved Sundew, Scarlet Pimpernel, Sea Mayweed, Sea Rocket, Sea-milkwort, Selfheal, Silverweed, Slender St. John's-wort, Spear Thistle, Square-stalked St. John's-wort, Thread-leaved Water-crowfoot, Thrift, Tufted Forget-me-not, Wall Speedwell, Water-cress, White Clover, Wild Pansy, Wild Thyme, Yellow-rattle.

Simon Wellock:

Amphibious Bistort, Bell Heather, Bloody Crane's-bill, Burnet Rose, Common Dog-violet, Common Juniper, Common Knapweed, Common Ragwort, Common Spotted- orchid, Common Stork's-bill, Common Twayblade, Cow Parsley, Cross-leaved Heath, Dove's-foot Crane's-bill, Early Marsh-orchid, Early-purple Orchid, Euphrasia heslop harrisonii, Frog Orchid, Groundsel, Harebell, Heath Fragrant-orchid, Heath Spotted-orchid, Heather, Hogweed, Irish Lady's-tresses, Lesser Butterfly-orchid, Long-headed Poppy, Marsh Ragwort, Northern Marsh orchid, Pineappleweed, Pipewort, Pyramidal Orchid, Red Bartsia, Red Dead-nettle, Redshank, Roseroot, Shepherd's-purse, Spotted Rock-rose, Tansy, Water Lobelia, White Water-lily, Wild Angelica, Wild Carrot.

Photographic credits

The letter after a page number refers to the order the image appears on that page, as though you were reading text. The letter a refers to the first image (highest and most left on the page), b the next image along and then down the page, etc.. Leaf scans are excluded.

John Bowler:
6a, 6b, 22a, 22b, 23a, 24a, 24b, 26a, 27a, 27b, 29, 30, 34b, 36a, 39a, 40b, 43c, 47b, 48b, 49, 53, 54a, 54b, 55, 56b, 60c, 61b, 62a, 62b, 66a, 66b, 72a, 73, 74a, 75a, 79a, 80, 81a, 82b, 84a, 84b, 87a, 87b, 88a, 89, 90a, 90b, 92b, 93a, 98b, 101b, 107a, 107b, 108a, 115a, 115b, 115c, 117a, 119a, 119b, 124a, 126, 129b, 130, 134b, 137a, 137b, 142a, 143c, 144a, 145a, 148a, 149a, 151a, 153b, 157a, 157b, 158a, 159a, 159b, 164b, 166a, 166b, 169a, 70b, 173

Freddie Everett:
14, 23b, 25a, 48a, 51, 63a, 83, 88b, 94a, 94b, 95a, 95b, 100a, 109b, 129a, 131a, 187b

Lynne Farrell:
82a, 104b, 140c, 161b

Lorne Gill/SNH:
26b, 38a, 61a, 64c, 97, 128a

Emma Grant:
20b, 25b, 65b, 67, 70b, 74b, 93b, 105a, 109a, 110b, 112b, 116c, 132a, 139a, 141b, 143b, 143d, 156b, and all leaf scans

Neil Mackinnon:
35b, 105b, 118b, 131b

Tony Oliver:
front cover, i, iv, 4, 5a, 5b, 7, 8a, 8b, 9, 11, 12, 15a, 15b, 19, 20a, 21a, 21b, 28, 31a, 31b, 32a, 32b, 33a, 34a, 35a, 36b, 37, 38b, 39b, 40a, 41, 42, 43a, 43b, 44, 45b, 46a, 46b, 47a, 50a, 50b, 52a, 52b, 56a, 57, 58, 59, 60a, 60b, 63b, 64a, 64b, 65a, 68, 69a, 69b, 71, 72b, 72c, 75b, 76, 77a, 77b, 78a, 79b, 81b, 85b, 85c, 86a, 91a, 91b, 92a, 98a, 99, 100b, 101a, 102a, 102b, 104a, 106a, 106b, 108b, 110a, 111a, 111b, 112a, 113a, 113b, 113b, 114, 116a, 116b, 117b, 119c, 120, 121a, 121b, 122, 123a, 123b, 124b, 125a, 125b, 127, 133a, 133b, 134a, 135a, 135b, 136a, 136b, 138a, 138b, 139b, 140a, 140b, 141a, 142b, 143a, 144b, 145a, 146, 147a, 147b, 148b, 150a, 150b, 151b, 152a, 152b, 153a, 154a, 154b, 155, 156a, 158b – 159, 160a, 160b, 161a, 162, 163a, 164a, 165a, 165b, 167, 168a, 168b, 169b, 170a, 171, 172, 174, 187a, back cover

Sarah Rose:
45a, 96a, 118a, 132b

Simon Wellock:
33b, 45c, 78b, 86b, 103a, 103b, 128b, 149b, 163b

Doug Young:
70a, 85a, 96b